The 'Way-Out, Wonderful World
of Horror, Fantasy and Sci-Fi
Movie Trivia

The 'Way-Out, Wonderful World of Horror, Fantasy and Sci-Fi Movie Trivia

by Keith Hedges

Copyright © 2007 Keith Hedges
Interior layout and cover design by Susan Svehla

Without limiting the rights under copyright reserved above, no part of this publication may be reproduced, stored in or introduced into a retrieval system, or transmitted, in any form, or by any means (electronic, mechanical, photocopying, recording, or otherwise), without the prior written permission of the copyright owners or the publishers of the book.
ISBN 10: 1-887664-75-0
ISBN 13: 978-1-887664-75-2
Library of Congress Catalog Card Number
Manufactured in the United States of America
First Printing by Midnight Marquee Press, Inc., May 2007
Second Printing by Midnight Marquee Press, Inc., September 2007

This book is dedicated to Forry Ackerman
and the millions of monster kids who grew up on
Famous Monsters of Filmland.
Thanks for giving us the "beast" years of our lives.

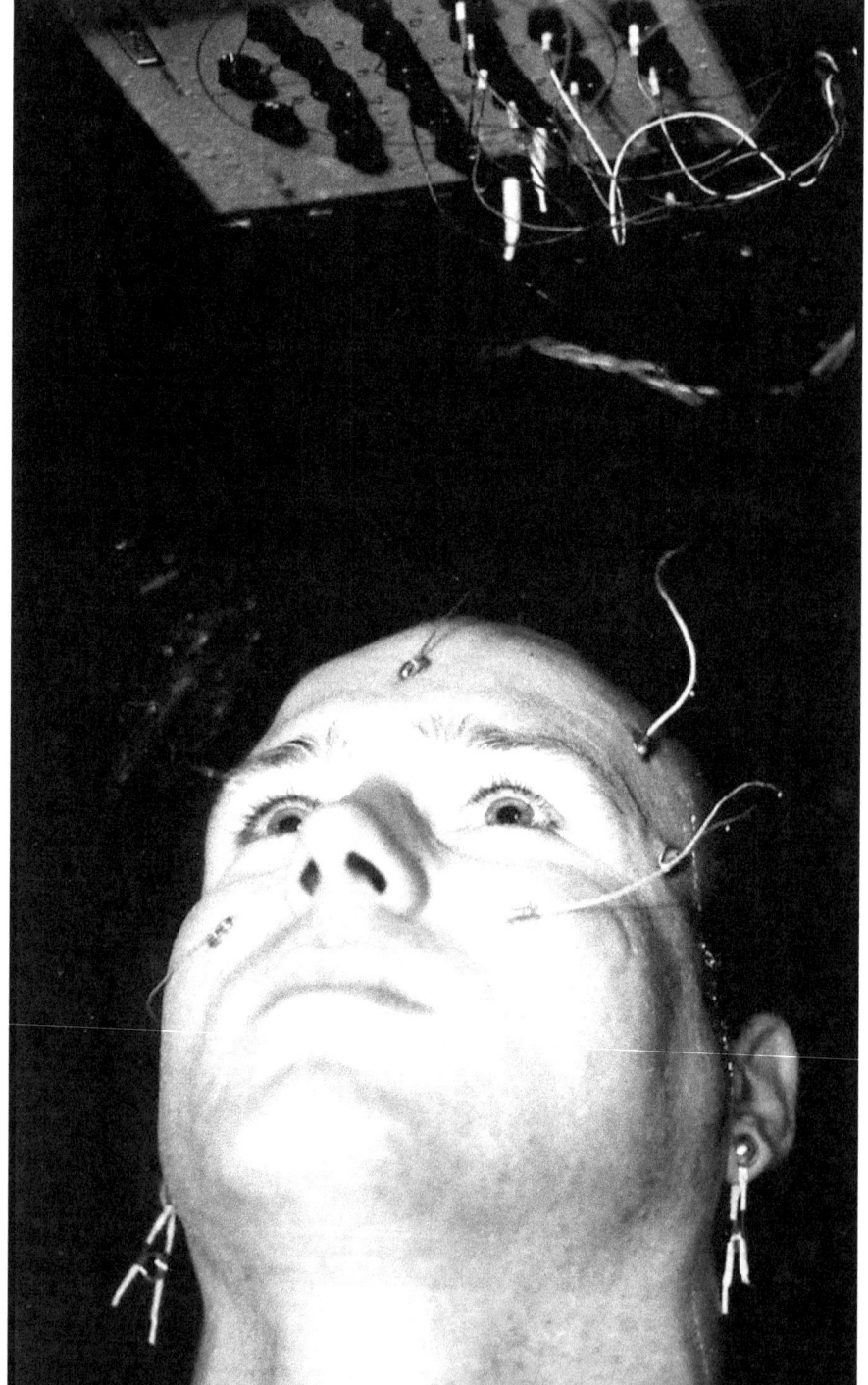

Table of Contents

9   Introduction

12   Test Your Monster IQ

130   Bibliography/Source Materials

131   Answer Pages

145   About the Author

Acknowledgments

First and foremost I'd like to thank my dear Lord for His gracious love in saving me and for the talents He has given me. For my lovely wife Elaine and my precious little son Donald, thank you for your patience and understanding in those times when I was typing away at the keyboard.

A special thanks to Susan Svehla for her support in putting all this together. Thanks to Anthony Ambrogio for his help on this project. To Jim Clatterbaugh (*Monsters from the Vault*) for the Elvis Wolfman photo from Fanex16, a great shot, thanks.

For my friend Abel Mills for his long-standing friendship and his knowledge of this genre. Thanks for being a sounding board for all those trivial questions.

To Midnight Marquee Press for believing in this project and publishing it.

And finally to those who purchased a copy and share the same kind of passion for those lovable old monster films, my deepest appreciation. Enjoy!

Introduction

For those of you reading this introduction—my fondest thanks. I grew up in the small town of Indian Head, Maryland. Here, in the pages of a kids' monster mag, I discovered a sense of wonder and imagination. A childhood hobby that grew into a lifelong obsession with classic horror films, those wondrous creatures of the silver screen.

For me during the 1960s, life was a seemingly simpler time—*The Outer Limits* said there was nothing wrong with our television set; Adam West was Batman; and Elvis could be found rocking out at your local drive-in.

As with most baby boomer monster fans, I found respite and comfort in those monsters flickering on the television screen.

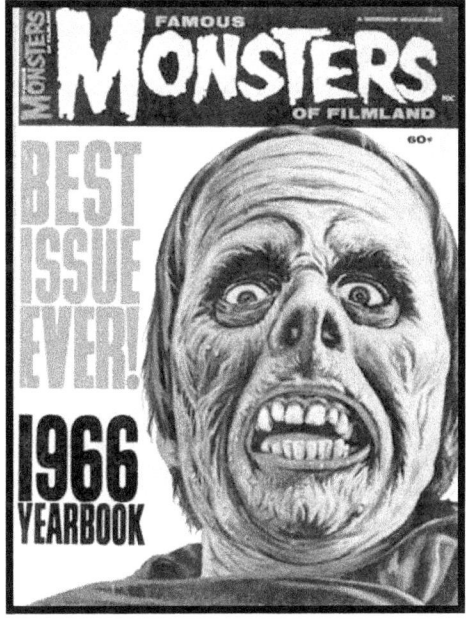

Of course aiding and abetting this obsession was *Famous Monsters of Filmland*. The first cherished issue I discovered was the 1966 Yearbook, which I picked up at a local shop. The mag featured that greenish glow of the *Phantom of the Opera*. It just begged me to pick it up and take it home. Not only were the pictures delightfully horrific, but the ads in the back offered so many more gruesome treats—monster masks, 8mm monster films and those great Aurora model kits from *Dracula* to *Frankenstein*. I purchased the model kits from the local Peoples Drug Store and my brother (the artistic one) was there to help build and paint these fabulous kits for me.

The local candy counter also offered a wide assortment of monstrous items—fanged wax teeth, orange witch wax harmonicas, monster wax figures with sweetened juice in them, and my favorite item of all—the bubble gum cards.

I remember happily chewing that hard stick of gum while looking at my favorite cards—Terror Tales. These had a funny blurb and an AIP monster scene on the front, and on the back was a story—supposedly true—called "Did It Ever Happen?"

One of the first monster films I really remember seeing was *Abbott and Costello Meet Frankenstein*, which was shown on our local Channel 9 (WTOP), and was hosted by Sir Graves Ghastly (Lawson Deming). It was here that I discovered all the Universal horror classics and not-so-classics like *Attack of the Mushroom People*.

My sister and I would haunt the local movie theater The Glymont, where we saw movies like *Viva Las Vegas* with Elvis Presley and *Frankenstein Conquers the World*. Eventually, I braved the darkened domain on my own to see a film called *Planet of the*

Apes. Only one or two movies played at the theater after that film, and then it suffered the same fate of most movie palaces–destruction in the name of progress.

My thirst for all things monstrous led me to other treasures as well. If *Famous Monsters* was not expected to appear anytime soon in the mailbox, I would purchase books on horror films. The very first title I found was *A Pictorial History of Horror Films* by Denis Gifford.

In the early 1970s, I would spend Saturday nights with Count Gore DeVol (Dick Dyszel), WDCA TV's Channel 20 *Creature Feature* horror host. The Count would offer classic horror/sci-fi films mixed with his campy humor that tickled my funny bone.

It wasn't till the amazing invention of home VCRs that I found horror heaven; now I could actually watch my monster movies any time I felt like it.

There is one other fanboy movie monster memory that I've come to cherish. It was the summer of 1993 in Towson, Maryland that I found a film convention called FANEX. It was here, through the gracious founders (Sue and Gary Svehla), that I was able to meet many of the fabulous stars, directors and special-effects wizards who gave us these memorable films. Attending FANEX, I have been able to meet Ray Harryhausen, the lovely actresses Veronica Carlson, Linda Harrison and Ingrid Pitt, Uncle Forry (*FM*'s own editor) and even Count Gore DeVol. And in a Monster Kid dream come true, I've had the chance to be on stage and sing with Count Gore himself (I make my living as an Elvis Presley impersonator—well, that's another story).

So there you have it, the brief history of a monster fan. So why a trivia book on monster movies when today you have the monster world at your fingertips? I guess there's still a little bit of a monster kid in all of us. And I've had a lifelong dream of

Forry Ackerman visited Count Gore's WDCA dungeon in 1984.

doing something to honor those monster movies that were so dear to me during my childhood. Even though I'm now 47, I'll always be a child at heart.

So grab the popcorn, and maybe if you time it just right, one dark and stormy night you can revel in those glorious memories of your monster-filled youth. A creaking door slowly opens and beckons you into *The 'Way-Out, Wonderful World of Horror, Fantasy and Sci-Fi Trivia.*
—Keith Hedges

For those super-smart fanboys and fangirls, can you identify the photos without captions? Answers on page 138.

TEST YOUR MONSTER IQ

Abbott and Costello Meet Frankenstein

1. What was the original title for the film?
2. Who was rumored to have been offered first choice to play Dracula? This was later disproved by Lugosi biographer Arthur Lennig.
3. True or false: Lon Chaney, Jr. also played the Frankenstein monster in one sequence in the film.
4. What apparent blooper is found in the film?
5. True or false: Leonard Maltin called it "the all-time great horror comedy."
6. Lenore Aubert (Sandra) also starred in another A & C film. Can you name it?
7. What is the name of the wax museum that receives the bodies of Frankenstein's Monster and Dracula?
8. Jane Randolph (Joan) appeared in two Val Lewton films. Name the films.
9. True or false: Elvis Presley was a big fan of the film.
10. What is the name Dracula uses in the film?
11. Who was originally slated for the role of Sandra?
12. Who supposedly said, "that Abbott and Costello made buffoons of the monsters"?
13. In the final few seconds of the film, what Universal monster gives Bud and Lou a scare?
14. What horror film star refused to see the picture but appeared in two other A & C horror comedies?

Answers page 131

The 'Way-Out, Wonderful World

Abbott and Costello Match

Match Bud and Lou's character names from their Sci-Fi, Fantasy, and Horror comedies. Extra: Match their name with its film title

1. Chick Young
2. Lou Francis
3. Chuck Murray
4. Freddy Phillips
5. Cuthbert Greenway/Dr. Robert Greenway
6. Peter Patterson
7. Casey Edwards
8. Orvil
9. Ferdinand Jones
10. Tubby
11. Bud Alexander
12. Wilbur Gray
13. Slim
14. Horatio Prim
15. Lester
16. Freddie Franklin

A) Hold That Ghost
B) Abbott and Costello Meet Dr. Jekyll and Mr. Hyde
C) Abbott and Costello Meet the Mummy
D) The Time of Their Lives
E) Abbott and Costello Meet Frankenstein
F) Abbott and Costello Go to Mars
G) Abbott and Costello Meet the Killer Boris Karloff
H) Abbott and Costello Meet the Invisible Man

Answers page 131

AKA
Match the actor/actress with their actual names

1. Bela Blasko
2. Beatrice Peterson
3. William Henry Pratt
4. Lawrence Rory Guy
5. Roger Engell
6. Nicolai Yoshkin
7. Vladimir Palanuik
8. Burnu Davenport
9. Elizabeth Sullivan
10. R.L. Hanks
11. Louis Albert Denninger, Jr.
12. Rauff de Ryther Duan Acklom
13. John Peter Richmond (has some credits under his real name)
14. Ladislav Loewenstein

A) Hillary Brooke
B) Martin Kosleck
C) Jack Palance
D) Zandor Vorkov
E) Elsa Lanchester
F) Angus Scrimm
G) Acquanetta
H) Boris Karloff
I) Robert Lowery
J) David Manners
K) Richard Denning
L) Bela Lugosi
M) John Carradine
N) Peter Lorre

Answers page 139

Alien Races
Match each alien race with its movie title in which it appeared

1. The Eloi
2. The Krel
3. The Davannans
4. Zahgons
5. Rehtonites
6. Venusians
7. Martians
8. Jawas
9. The Selenites
10. Saturnians
11. Sumerians

A) The Mole People
B) This Island Earth
C) The Phantom Planet
D) Queen of Outer Space
E) The Three Stooges in Orbit
F) Forbidden Planet
G) Star Wars
H) Not of This Earth
I) First Men in the Moon
J) The Time Machine
K) Buck Rogers

Answers page 139

of Horror, Fantasy and Sci-Fi Movie Trivia   15

Alternate Film Titles
Match each original film title with its alternate title

1. Invasion of the Saucer Men
2. The Two Faces of Dr. Jekyll
3. Frankenstein's Daughter
4. The Manster
5. The Creeping Unknown
6. The Creeping Terror
7. Invasion of the Body Snatchers
8. The Fearless Vampire Killers
9. The Magic Sword
10. The Invisible Ghost
11. The Time of Their LiveS
12. Blood of Dracula
13. The Horror of Party Beach
14. Dracula vs. Frankenstein
15. Monster from the Ocean Floor
16. Gamera vs. Outer Space MonsterViras

A) The Split
B) Sleep No More
C) Spacemen Saturday Night
D) House of Fright
E) Destroy All Planets
F) She Monster of the Night
G) The Phantom Killer
H) The Quatermass Xperiment
I) Dangerous Charter
J) Dance of the Vampires
K) Invasion of the Zombies
L) Blood of Frankenstein
M) Blood is My Heritage
N) Monster Maker
O) St. George and the Dragon
P) The Ghost Steps Out

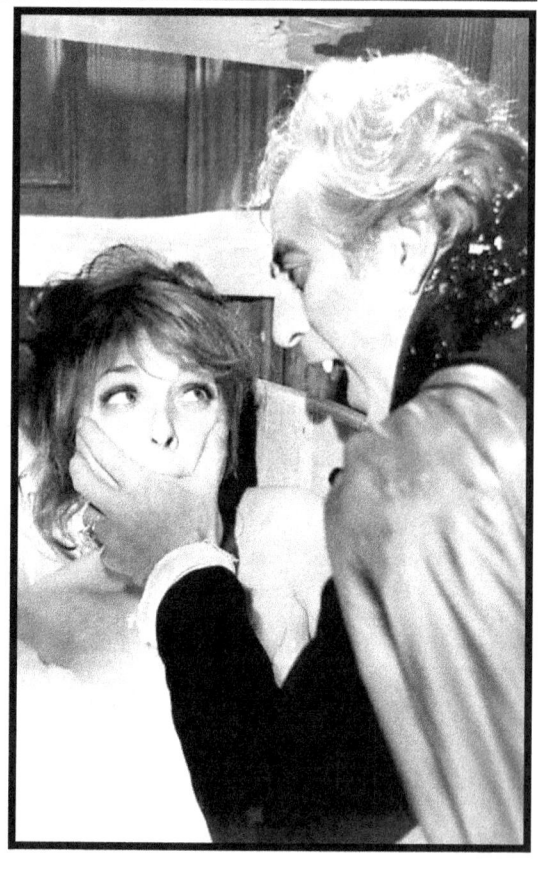

Answers page 139

Amazing Heroes
Match each hero with their profile

1. Michael Crawford is a cartoonist who creates a comic book hero that he emulates
2. King Brothers feature about an Arabian swashbuckler
3. Marvel comic book hero fights a villain named Scarab
4. Robert Lowery played this crusader in a 15-chapter serial
5. The Spider Lady is the villainess in this Sam Katzman serial starring Kirk Alyn
6. This serial crime fighter was based on a pulp series and starred Warren Hull
7. Victor Jory is the dark avenger in this 15-chapter serial
8. Steve Reeves is the sword and sandal hero trying to regain his memory
9. Fawcett comic book hero portrayed by Kane Richmond
10. Gordon Scott is out to destroy bloodsucking fiends
11. 1952 Republic serial starring Commando Cody
12. Comic strip cop is at odds against an invisible foe
13. Irish McCalla stars as this jungle heroine
14. Space hero fights a dragon lizard monster called a Gocko
15. Comic book jungle heroine played by Kay Aldridge
16. Space hero who was found suspended in animation
17. He fought the Jungle Moon Men
18. He helped Evelyn Ankers restore her youth
19. Johnny Sheffield starred in this series
20. Toby Maguire portrayed this amazing hero

A) Captain America
B) Superman
C) Bomba the Jungle Boy
D) The Spiders Web
E) Condorman
F) Hercules Unchained
G) Spy Smasher
H) Captain Sinbad
I) The Shadow
J) Tarzan
K) Batman
L) Goliath
M) Radar Men from the Moon
N) Dick Tracy vs. Crime Inc.
O) Sheena
P) Buck Rogers
Q) Flash Gordon
R) Nyoka
S) Jungle Jim
T) Spiderman

Answers page 139

Artists and Monsters

Monster films owe a great debt to the artists who conceive and create imaginary creatures for the celluloid film. Here are but a few who have given us sheer delight in the unusual. Match the following make-up artists with their profile.

1. Make-up effects for House of Dark Shadows
2. Assembled The Monster of Piedras Blancas
3. Make-up artist for 1931's Dr. Jekyll and Mr. Hyde
4. Make-up artist worked on many simian films
5. Won Special Achievement Award on Total Recall
6. Universal's chief make-up artist
7. He's a British make-up artist at Hammer Studios.
8. Known as "the man of a thousand faces"
9. Special effects artist on Fright Night
10. Uncredited makeup artist on Charles Laughton's Quasimodo
11. Succeeded #6 answer at Universal Studios
12. Australian who worked on The Curse of the Werewolf
13. Make-up artist on Frankenstein's Daughter
14. He provided make-up for the film Night Tide
15. He worked on Dawn of the Dead
16. He is associated with the Crypt Keeper

A) Lon Chaney
B) Bud Westmore
C) Harry Thomas
D) Rick Baker
E) Dick Smith
F) Jack Pierce
G) Rob Bottin
H) Jack Kevan
I) Perc Westmore
J) Phil Leakey
K) Roy Ashton
L) Wally Westmore
M) Steve Johnson
N) Tom Savini
O) Bruno Ve Sota
P) Kevin Yagher

Answers page 139

Assorted Horrors

1. In what film did Michael Pate portray a gun-slinging vampire?
2. Jethro of Beverly Hillbillies fame's uncle starred in a movie involving a giant conquistador. Can you name it?
3. Faith Domergue starred in what film that involved a curse and several stars of classic TV shows?
4. Who played Mario in The Spider Woman Strikes Back?
5. Name the Monogram film that featured a ghostly lady and her Great Dane, both of whom can walk through walls.
6. King Kong's leading lady, Fay Wray, also appeared in at least six other films in the genre. Can you name them?
7. Who played the ghost of Mary Meredith in The Uninvited?
8. Name the film that was originally entitled I Was a Teenage Gorilla
9. In the film Blackbeard's Ghost, what is the name of Blackbeard's wife, who placed a curse on him?
10. What 1967 film had Akim Tamiroff as a man with a body, wings and legs of a bird?
11. A woman suspects her husband is an alien from outer space. Can you name the film?
12. A man takes on simian qualities after being cursed by a witch. (Hint: Curt Siodmak directed the film.) Can you name it?
13. Name the film where a campus professor becomes a Neanderthal caveman.
14. British sci-fi film about a husband discovering his wife is an alien sent to kill scientists and their space project. Can you name the film?
15. In what film do you find giant African wasps terrorizing a scientific research expedition?
16. Name the film where two scientists clone a beautiful woman they both love
17. A mad scientist creates amoeba-like monsters that attack castaways. What is the film?
18. Country artist Kortney Kale's music video tune "Don't Let Me Down" features an Allied Artist sci-fi classic on the tube. Can you name it?
19. What 1960s girl group sings the theme song for "Dr. Goldfoot and the Bikini Machine"?
20. In the film "Buck Privates Come Home" what horror poster is seen in the background on the bus? (Hint: It's a British film)
21. In what film did Bud Abbott and Lou Costello meet Margaret Hamilton (the Wicked Witch from The Wizard of Oz) brewing up a love potion for Lou?
22. What dinosaur film holds the title of being the most used as stock footage for many films and TV shows?
23. What controversy is still seething to this day regarding this dinosaur film?

Answers page 131

B-Movie Greats

What would those great B 1950s/1960s sci-fi/horror films be without the actors and actresses who took on the monsters.

1. Mr. Perkins (Blood of Dracula)
2. Seymour (The Little Shop of Horrors)
3. Dr. Kettering (The Brain Eaters)
4. Sheriff Cagle (Earth vs. the Spider)
5. Tom Stevens (The Day the Earth Stood Still)
6. Dave Walker (Attack of the Giant Leeches)
7. Mitch McAffee (The Giant Claw)
8. Dr. Alfred Brandon (I Was a Teenage Werewolf)
9. Stephanie Clayton (Tarantula)
10. Dr. Le Farge (The Mole People)
11. Dr. Carrington (The Thing from Another World)
12. Colonel Evans (The Beast from 20,000 Fathoms)
13. Eric (The Screaming Skull)
14. Joyce (War of the Colossal Beast)
15. Enger (Viking Women and the Sea Serpent)
16. Kelston (Invaders from Mars)
17. Sally (Attack of the Puppet People)
18. Rostov (Lost Continent)
19. Kingman (Earth vs. the Spider)
20. Livia (The Undead)
21. Stefan (The Terror)
22. Stern (Kronos)
23. Jim Maddison (Day the World Ended)
24. Robert Scott Carey (The Incredible Shrinking Man)
25 Dr. Meades (Man from Planet X)

Answers page 139

A) Morris Ankrum
B) John Hudson
C) Gene Roth
D) Arthur Franz
E) Whit Bissell
F) Hugh Marlowe
G) Sally Fraser
H) June Kenney
I) Ed Nelson
J) Thomas B. Henry
K) William Shallert
L) Jeff Morrow
M) Ed Kemmer
N) Dick Miller
O) Jonathan Haze
P) Paul Birch
Q) Bruno Ve Sota
R) Mara Corday
S) Nestor Paiva
T) Kenneth Tobey
U) John Hoyt
V) Susan Cabot
W) Robert Cornthwaite
X) Allison Hayes
Y) Grant Williams

Ballyhoo

Showmanship on a grand scale was used to promote horror/sci-fi and fantasy flicks. Those fascinating gimmicks hold fond memories for those who were there for the excitement.

1. The first 10,000 people to see this film received a set of black stamps
2. Female patrons receive a pair of cutout zombie eyes
3. Male audiences receive a pair of cutout fangs
4. Illusion-O — ghostviewers were given to patrons
5. A small poster is handed to patrons
6. Percepto — theater seats are hot-wired
7. Emergo — a floating skeleton overhead
8. Lloyds of London insures for $1,000 if anyone scared to death
9. Hypnovista promotes this film
10. Punishment Poll — audiences vote on the end of the film
11. Subliminal messages flash before your eyes
12. Patrons receive a cardboard axe with fake blood
13. Take a fright break/have blood pressure checked
14. An audience patron could receive $50,000 from an insurance company if patron proved the movie's monster was not on Mars
15. Space Shield Protectors for prevention of being abducted into outer space were given to patrons in the theater
16. Packets of green blood are given to American audiences
17. Free engagement ring to female patrons

A) The Horrors of the Black Museum
B) 13 Ghosts
C) Homicidal
D) House on Haunted Hill
E) Terror in the Haunted House
F) The Curse of the Mummy's Tomb
G) Matinee
H) Macabre
I) Frankenstein Meets the Space Monster
J) The Tingler
K) Plague of the Zombies
L) Mr. Sardonicus
M) It! The Terror from Beyond Space
N) Strait-Jacket
O) Dracula — Prince of Darkness
P) Vampire People
Q) Brides of Blood

Answers page 139

of Horror, Fantasy and Sci-Fi Movie Trivia

Behind the Screams

Let us pay homage to some of the artists behind the scenes, who gave us those astounding camera angles, bizarre sets and great special effects during the golden age of Horrorwood.

1. John J. Mescall
2. Charles D. Hall
3. Arthur Edeson
4. Karl Struss
5. Karl Freund
6. Cedric Gibbons
7. John P. Fulton
8. Edgar G. Ulmer
9. Charles Stumar
10. Russell A. Gausman
11. Kenneth Strickfadden
12. James Wong Howe
13. Arthur Martinelli

A) Art director for The Mask of Fu Manchu/Mad Love
B) Cinematographer on Frankenstein
C) Set designer on M
D) Cinematographer on The Mummy and The Raven
E) Cinematographer on Bride of Frankenstein
F) Art director on Dracula/Frankenstein
G) Special effects on The Invisible Man
H) Cinematographer on Dracula
I) Cinematographer on Dr. Jekyll and Mr. Hyde
J) Cinematographer for Mark of the Vampire
K) Set decorator on Son of Frankenstein
L) Director of photography on White Zombie
M) Electrical effects contributor on Bride of Frankenstein

Answers page 139

Body Parts
Match each film title with its body part plot

1. An old spinster wants her brain transplanted into a young girl
2. A doctor saves his fiancée's head while searching for a suitable body
3. An evil brain from another planet possesses a nuclear physicist
4. A 300-year-old monster uses his tongue to suck out the brains of its victims
5. An astronaut's severed hand controls a teenage boy
6. A murdered pianist's hand seeks vengeance
7. A preserved brain of a business tycoon plays mind games with Lew Ayres
8. A deadly gas, kidnappings, and preserving a live head are in the plot
9. A black convict and a racist white surgeon find themselves attached to each other
10. A murderer's hands are grafted onto a pianist
11. A buried chest containing the head of an evil sorcerer seeks to find its body
12. Creatures below the Earth bore into their victims' necks to control their minds
13. A doctor transforms a man into a two-headed creature
14. Mountain climbers are killed in the Alps by a giant-sized body part
15. An alien hand tries to inject alcohol into two teenagers
16. A head of an evil ancient warrior is alive

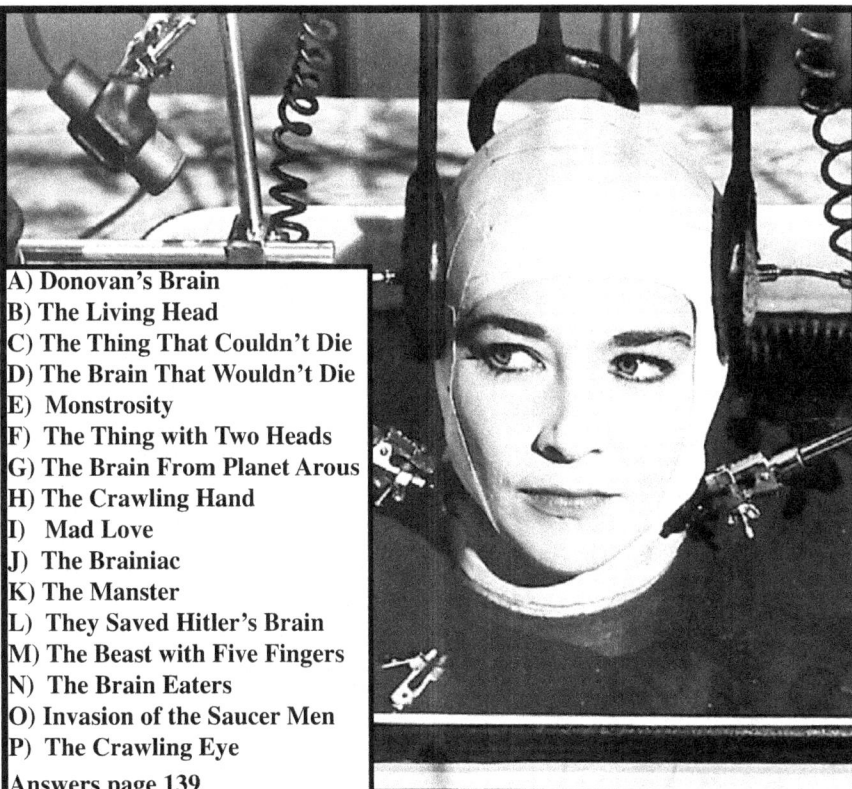

A) Donovan's Brain
B) The Living Head
C) The Thing That Couldn't Die
D) The Brain That Wouldn't Die
E) Monstrosity
F) The Thing with Two Heads
G) The Brain From Planet Arous
H) The Crawling Hand
I) Mad Love
J) The Brainiac
K) The Manster
L) They Saved Hitler's Brain
M) The Beast with Five Fingers
N) The Brain Eaters
O) Invasion of the Saucer Men
P) The Crawling Eye

Answers page 139

The Boys Are Back in Town

Match each Bowery Boys and East Side Kids movie with its plot synopsis

1. Magician Lugosi in an old mansion
2. The boys exterminate a mad scientist's house
3. Glenn Strange as Atlas in need of a brain
4. A ghost helps the boys with phony mediums
5. Hypnosis turns Huntz Hall into a super boxer
6. The boys come across a Genie in Aladdin's lamp
7. Nazi spy (Lugosi) haunts an old house
8. Huntz Hall becomes a super-strength wrestler
9. An old house, lost loot and a claw-handed ghost
10. Huntz Hall is a singing sensation due to tonsillitis
11. An old mansion, & graveyard and tiptoeing ghost
12. Huntz Hall makes a vitamin that turns him into a football star
13. Boys seek strange owners for vacant lot for local kids' baseball park

A) Mr. Hex
B) Spook Chasers
C) Hold That Line
D) Master Minds
E) Spooks Run Wild
F) The Bowery Boys Meet the Monsters
G) No Holds Barred
H) Ghosts on the Loose
I) Bowery to Bagdad
J) Spook Busters
K) Ghost Chasers
L) Blues Busters
M) Boys of the City

Answers page 139

24   The 'Way-Out, Wonderful World

Cartoon Creeps
Identify the following cartoons with their TV series or name.

1. Spinoff cartoon from the Archies series
2. Jodie Foster provided one of the voices for this group who travel in a haunted motor home
3. This series was based on a Japanese comic book
4. Tim Matheson was the voice for this daring lad
5. Cartoon creature created by Professor Weirdo
6. You'll meet Little Tibia and the Phibias here
7. He unravels mysteries with the help of a snack
8. Rankin Bass series with Prof. Bond & family
9. Max Fleischer produced seventeen cartoons based on this character.
10. A boy named Buzz and his 30-foot robot
11. Vincent Price is Ratigan the rat
12. Starred in "Hair-Raising Hare"
13. Gary Owens supplied his voice
14. He played Dr. Frankenstein
15. What cartoon characters have the name Weirdly and Creepella?
16. Monsters attend a wedding celebration
17. Where can you find a cartoon character named Frankencelery?

A) Astro Boy
B) Veggie Tales
C) Mad Mad Mad Monsters
D) The Addams Family
E) Groovie Goolies
F) Jonny Quest
G) The Great Mouse Detective
H) Mad Monster Party
I) Scooby Doo Where Are You?
J) Mr. Magoo
K) Frankenstein, Jr.
L) The Gruesomes
M) Superman
N) Bugs Bunny
O) Space Ghost
P) Milton the Monster
Q) King Kong

Answers page 139

of Horror, Fantasy and Sci-Fi Movie Trivia

Composing Thoughts

Match each composer with his or her profile

1. Wrote theme for The Thing from Another World
2. German composer for Bride of Frankenstein
3. Austrian composer well remembered for the symphonic score for King Kong
4. Introduced us to electronic planetary sounds in the Forbidden Planet
5. British composer associated with Hammer Films including The Curse of Frankenstein
6. Composer for many Universal features including Creature from the Black Lagoon
7. American composer on Roger Corman's Edgar Allan Poe films
8. Wrote theme song for The Addams Family
9. Scored the music for Abbott and Costello Meet Frankenstein
10. American composer for RKO Radio Pictures including Cat People and Mighty Joe Young
11. Scored several Alfred Hitchcock films
12. Composed the score for the 1940 fantasy classic The Thief of Bagdad
13. Composed the score for Experiment in Terror
14. Composer for Star Wars, Jurassic Park and ET

A) John Williams
B) Frank Skinner
C) Hans J. Salter
D) Miklos Rozsa
E) Bernard Herrmann
F) Vic Mizzy
G) James Bernard
H) Henry Mancini
I) Dimitri Tiomkin
J) Louis and Bebe Barron
K) Max Steiner
L) Franz Waxman
M) Les Baxter
N) Roy Webb

Answers page 139

Creature Features/Double Features
Match each film with its double feature counterpart

1. The Ghost and Mr. Chicken
2. The Screaming Skull
3. Zombies of Mora Tau
4. The Alligator People
5. Attack of the Puppet People
6. Horror of Party Beach
7. She Wolf of London
8. The Day the World Ended
9. Die Monster Die
10. The Crawling Hand
11. The Giant Gila Monster
12. I Was a Teenage Werewolf
13. I Was a Teenage Frankenstein
14. The Cyclops
15. Indestructible Man
16. The Undead
17. The Raven
18. How to Make a Monster
19. The Astounding She Monster
20. Attack of the Giant Leeches
21. Earth vs. the Flying Saucers
22. The Return of Dracula
23. The Snake Woman
24. The Wasp Woman
25. The Monster That Challenged the World
26. Attack of the Crab Monsters

A) The Cat Creeps
B) The Vampire
C) War of the Colossal Beast
D) Planet of the Vampires
E) Not of this Earth
F) The Slime People
G) Terror in the Year 5000
H) World Without End
I) The Killer Shrews
J) Return of the Fly
K) Invasion of the Saucer Men
L) Daughter of Dr. Jekyll
M) Blood of Dracula
N) Night Tide
O) Teenage Caveman
P) Voodoo Woman
Q) Munster Go Home
R) A Bucket of Blood
S) Dr. Blood's Coffin
T) The Werewolf
U) The Flame Barrier
V) Beast from the Haunted Cave
W) Phantom from 10,000 Leagues
X) The Man Who Turned to Stone
Y) The Curse of the Living Corpse
Z) The Viking Women and the Sea Serpent

Answers page 140

Creepy Houses and Spooky Locations
Match each film with its sinister location

1. House of Long Shadows
2. Son of Dracula
3. Psycho
4. And Then There Were None
5. Salem's Lot
6. Dark Shadows (TV)
7. Munster Go Home
8. Lady in White
9. The Uninvited
10. The Fog
11. The Haunting
12. The Ghost and Mr. Chicken
13. Bride of the Monster
14. Dracula
15. Die Monster Die
16. King Kong
17. Horror Hotel
18. Giant from the Unknown
19. The Ghost Breakers
20. The Munsters (TV)
21. The Midnight Hour
22. Curse of the Demon
23. Dr. X

A) 1313 Mockingbird Lane
B) Hill House
C) Windwood House
D) Antonio Bay
E) Marsten House
F) Bald Pate Manor
G) Bates Motel
H) Indian Island
I) Dark Oaks
J) Munster Hall
K) Carfax Abbey
L) Skull Island
M) White Wood
N) Black Island
O) Devil's Crag
P) Simmons Mansion
Q) Willow Point Falls
R) Witley House
S) The Old Willows Place
T) Lufford Hall
U) Widow's Hill
W) Pitchford Cove
X) Blackstone Shoals

Answers page 140

Creature from the Black Lagoon

1. Who is known as the original Gillman?
2. Who played the underwater creature in the creature trilogy?
3. Can you name the three creature films in the order that they were made?
4. Who played the creature on land in the second film?
5. Name the three actresses who were menaced by the creature from each film
6. Who played the creature on land in the third film?
7. Clint Eastwood made his film debut in which creature film?
8. The creature made the cover of what automobile magazine?
9. What show with Abbott and Costello did the creature appear on?
10. Who originally was considered for the role of the creature in the first film?
11. What process was used for two of the creature films?
12. Who directed the first two films?
13. True or false: In 1971 an aquarium toy of the creature was released.
14. In what film that featured Marilyn Monroe did she express her sorrow for the creature?
15. Where were the location shots for Creature from the Black Lagoon filmed?
16. Who developed the concept drawings for the creature?
17. Name the boat that leads the expedition of scientists to the Black Lagoon
18. What is the captain's name?
19. Name the three composers who scored the soundtrack for the first film
20. The #2 answer, as well as playing the creature underwater, had a cameo as a lab assistant in which creature film?
21. The creature showed up on The Munsters in 1964 as one of their relatives. What was his name?
22. What film was the inspiration for Creature from the Black Lagoon?
23. What was used to tranquilize the creature in the first two films?

Answers page 131

Dino-Mania

1. Name the film in which a caveman, a Tyrannosaurus Rex and a Brontosaurus are awakened on a tropical island.
2. Name the 1959 Willis O'Brien film where a Brontosaurus is on the rampage in London.
3. Name the film where a flying Pterodactyl sends a helicopter down into a hot spot in the South Pole.
4. What Tarzan film would you find a giant spider, a dinosaur and Nazis in?
5. Name the film where a space crew is attacked by giant lizards on the planet Nova.
6. Richard Denning discovers prehistoric creatures and a giant sloth on an uncharted island. Can you name the film?
7. A couple of children raise five dinosaurs in this 1993 film that spawned two sequels. What is the film?
8. Patrick McGoohan pursues a baby Brontosaurus in this 1985 Disney feature. Name the film.
9. A rancher finds himself up against an evil land baron and a Tyrannosaurus Rex in what film?
10. An underground river takes four boys to a land of dinosaurs in this Czechoslovakian film. What is its title?
11. In what film would you find a cave girl mistaken for a baby dinosaur?

Answers page 132

Dracula

1. To whom does Dracula (Bela Lugosi) say, "I never drink wine"?
2. Who provided the voice for the unseen harbormaster in the 1931 Dracula?
3. What was the name of the 1922 silent version of Dracula that Bram Stoker's widow never gave permission to film?
4. Who portrays Dracula's Daughter in the 1936 Universal film?
5. In what film do you find Dracula posing as Count Alucard?
6. Name the 1958 British film that revived Bram Stoker's vampire
7. Though his name is provided in the title, what Hammer Dracula film never had Dracula in it?
8. What 1958 film had Dracula posing as an artist?
9. What 1965 Hammer film had Dracula putting the bite on Barbara Shelley?
10. Name the Hammer Dracula film poster campaign that shows an actress with a bandage on her neck
11. In what film does Dracula place a curse on an African prince?
12. Peter Cushing returned as Professor Van Helsing in what 1972 Dracula film?

Answers page 132

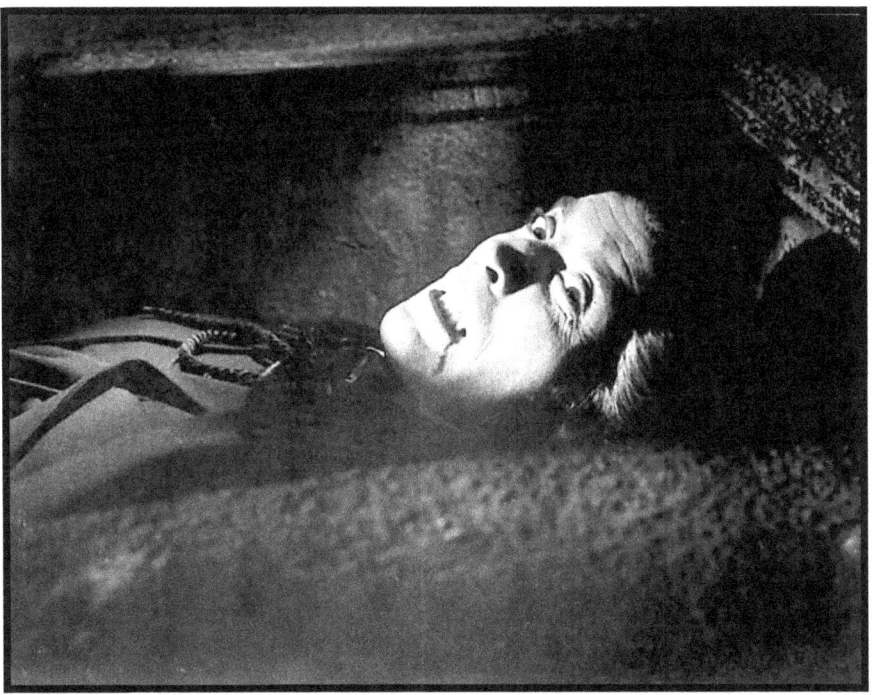

Family Ties
Can you match each celebrity with their family ties?

1. Mother was a United States Treasurer
2. Father was a British colonel
3. Father was a lawyer
4. Father was a meat packer
5. Father was the owner of a candy company
6. Father was a blast furnaceman
7. Sister was Jeanette MacDonald
8. Parents were circus employees
9. Father was a Greek merchant
10. Father was a tailor
11. Father was in engineering
12. Great grandfather fought against Napoleon at Waterloo
13. Father was an artist
14. Mother was an Arapaho Indian
15. Father was a deputy commissioner for the Salt Revenue Service in Bombay

A) Vincent Price
B) George Zucco
C) Bud Abbott
D) Pat Priest
E) Blossom Rock
F) Laird Cregar
G) Maria Ouspenskaya
H) Roger Corman
I) John Zacherle
K) Colin Clive
L) Peggy Moran
M) James Whale
N) John Agar
O) Boris Karloff
P) Burnu Acquanetta

Answers page 140

34　　　　The 'Way-Out, Wonderful World

Fantastic Phantoms
Match the following phantoms with their film titles

1. Bela Lugosi portrays Dr. Zorka in this 1939 Universal serial
2. 1956 film produced by the Milner brothers starring Cathy Downs and Kent Taylor
3. Catherine Zeta Jones appeared in this 1996 jungle adventure based on a comic strip character
4. 1970 fantasy about a boy in a magical world starring Butch Patrick
5. A rock palace is haunted by a phantom (William Finley)
6. Richard Kiel (Jaws from the James Bond films) plays a Solarite in this 1961 sci-fi flick
7. 1953 film about an invisible space alien
8. A movie studio is haunted by a phantom figure in this 1974 TV movie
9. Liam Neeson's sci-fi prequel to a classic science fiction film
10. A rock group helps an amusement park raise ticket sales while battling monstrous robotic creations by a mechanical wizard
11. Mary Philbin does her classic unmasking scene
12. Claude Rains knows the score

Answers page 140

A) The Phantom Planet
B) The Phantom of Hollywood
C) Phantom of the Paradise
D) Star Wars: Episode 1 — The Phantom Menace
E) Phantom from Space
F) Phantom from 10,000 Leagues
G) The Phantom Creeps
H) The Phantom
I) The Phantom Toll Booth
J) Phantom of the Opera (1925)
K) The Phantom of the Opera (1943)
L) Kiss Meets the Phantom of the Park

Film Stars With Elvis

Match the following horror stars who at one time or another have played opposite Elvis Presley. Some film titles are used several times.

1. Glenn Strange (House of Frankenstein)
2. John Carradine (House of Dracula)
3. Debra Paget (The Haunted Palace)
4. William Campbell (Dementia 13)
5. Vincent Price (The Pit and the Pendulum)
6. Charles Bronson (House of Wax)
7. Arthur O'Connell (The 7 Faces of Dr. Lao)
8. Jack Mullaney (Dr. Goldfoot and the Bikini Machine)
9. Nancy Sinatra (The Ghost in the Invisible Bikini)
10. Bruce Bennett (The Alligator People)
11. Wendell Corey (Astro-Zombies)
12. Angelique Petty John (Mad Doctor of Blood Island)
13. Barbara Eden (Voyage to the Bottom of the Sea)
14. Pat Priest (The Incredible Two Headed Transplant)
15. Carolyn Jones (Invasion of the Body Snatchers)
16. Dean Jagger (X—the Unknown)
17. Julie Adams (Creature from the Black Lagoon)
18. Anne Helm (The Magic Sword)
19. Joan Blackman (Visit to a Small Planet)
20. Yvonne Craig (Mars Needs Women)
21. Anthony Eisley (Dracula vs. Frankenstein)
22. Richard Carlson (It Came from Outer Space)
23. Ursula Andress (She)
24. Cesare Danova (Valley of the Dragons)
25. Leif Erickson (Invaders from Mars)
26. Yvonne Romaine (Curse of the Werewolf)

A) Tickle Me
B) Double Trouble
C) Jailhouse Rock
D) Love Me Tender
E) The Trouble With Girls
F) Follow That Dream
G) Kid Galahad
H) Blue Hawaii
I) Change of Habit
J) Fun in Acapulco
K) Speedway
L) Clambake
M) King Creole
N) Flaming Star
O) Kissin' Cousins
P) Viva Las Vegas
Q) Loving You
R) Easy Come Easy Go
S) Frankie and Johnny
T) Spinout
U) Roustabout

Answers page 140

Elvis with (Top to Bottom):
Joan Blackman
Ursula Andress
Debra Paget
Barbara Eden

For Monster Boomers Only

1. Who hosted *Shock Theatre* in Philadelphia as Roland?
2. What periodical premiered in February 1958?
3. In 1962 what model company produced a line of monster models?
4. What was the first monster model produced in 1962?
5. What song stayed on Billboard's #1 spot for two weeks?
6. Who were TV's first family of fright?
7. Name the slinky 1950s horror hostess
8. Name the extraterrestrial out of this world cereal
9. What television show premiered on September 18, 1964?
10. What television show opened with a silhouetted figure?
11. Name the 1966 gothic vampire who appeared on a daytime soap opera
12. Which Outer Limits episode was a pilot for a proposed series?
13. Name the horror actor who was slated for the role in the pilot but passed away before production started
14. In 1966 two model kits (The Vampire and The Frog) were created by what showman of horror films?
15. Name the long-playing novelty album of monster songs that originally was to feature Peter Lorre
16. Name the Canadian supernatural soap opera from 1969 that emulated Dark Shadows
17. Name the episode title from Route 66 that featured Karloff, Lorre and Lon Chaney, Jr.
18. Who created a line of classic monster masks and was featured in the pages of Famous Monsters?
19. What horror actor's mask has been the largest seller?
20. Name the five monster cereals from General Mills
21. Name the company that released condensed film versions of the Universal monsters on Super 8 and Regular 8 home movies
22. In 1957 on Ralph Edwards' This is Your Life, what horror legend was honored?
23. What's the name of the Gold Key comic book that pictured Boris Karloff on its cover?

24. Which Universal monster would you find riding in a Flivver in the plastic model series?
25. What's the name of the film playing on the drive-in screen in the opening sequence of the Hanna-Barbara Flintstones cartoon series?
26. In what AIP film would you find a teenager reading the first issue of Famous Monsters of Filmland?
27. Name the publishing company that produced such titles as Tales from the Crypt and The Vault of Horror
28. George Barris designed the Batmobile and numerous other cars in television's history. Name the two cars he customized for The Munsters TV series
29. Name the artist who did the cover box art for the Aurora monsters model kits in the early 1960s
30. What television show host introduced Zacherley by giving him the title "The Cool Ghoul"?
31. What furry creature dared you to look in his box from the mail order pages of FM?
32. What was the name of the mask featured in FM that also became a familiar image on their t-shirts?
33. Who was featured on the cover of Monster World #2 in January 1965?
34. What's the name of the very first set of monster cards that used classic monster photos on a slick glossy paper?

Answers page 132

Foreign Horrors
Match each film title with its foreign plot

1. Italy/France: A mad professor keeps his daughter alive with the blood of young girls and then uses their corpses as statues
2. Mexico: An artist is possessed by a 15th-century vampire
3. Mexico: A mad scientist turns sleepwalkers into museum pieces
4. England: An architect in Morocco is pursued by a vampire princess
5. Philippines: Vampire mad doctor pursues the twin sister of his dying wife for her heart
6. Spain: A professor becomes a werewolf after an expedition in Tibet
7. Mexico: A bearded vampire is a descendant of a 16th-century prophet
8. Italy: Gordon Scott battles zombies and a shape-changing vampire
9. Mexico: version of *Abbott and Costello Meet Frankenstein*
10. Japan: Reptile originally titled *Gojira*
11. England: A Frankenstein monster is used to catch young girls who are turned into mannequins
12. Mexico: Lon Chaney, Jr. is a mummy turned werewolf

Answers page 140

A) The Fury of the Wolfman
B) The Hand of Night
C) Castle of the Monsters
D) Samson in the Wax Museum
E) Vampire People
F) Mill of the Stone Women
G) Goliath and the Vampires
H) Track of the Vampire
I) The Blood of Nostradamus
J) Carry on Screaming
K) Godzilla King of the Monsters
L) Face of the Screaming Werewolf

Frankenstein By Any Other Name
Match the actors who portrayed the monster with their various film roles

1. Glenn Strange
2. Bela Lugosi
3. Boris Karloff
4. Charles Ogle
5. David Prowse
6. Kiwi Kingston
7. Christopher Lee
8. Lon Chaney, Jr.
9. Robert De Niro
10. Peter Boyle
11. Cal Bolder
12. Gary Conway
13. Mike Lane
14. Robert Reilly
15. Bo Swenson
16. Henry Wilson
17. Deron McBee

A) The Evil of Frankenstein
B) The Ghost of Frankenstein
C) How to Make a Monster
D) Frankenstein and the Monster From Hell
E) Jesse James Meets Frankenstein's Daughter
F) Curse of Frankenstein
G) Frankenstein Meets the Space Monster
H) Mary Shelley's Frankenstein
I) Frankenstein Meets the Wolfman
J) Frankenstein (1973)
K) Young Frankenstein
L) Frankenstein 1970
M) Bride of Frankenstein
N) Frankenstein's Daughter
O) Thomas Edison's 1910 version
P) Frankenstein Sings
Q) House of Frankenstein

Answers page 140

of Horror, Fantasy and Sci-Fi Movie Trivia

Game Show of Horrors

Match each spooky celebrity with the game show on which he or she appeared

1. He was a panelist on Quick As a Flash
2. Appeared on You Bet Your Life as a contestant
3. Said he was afraid of mice on I've Got A Secret
4. Appeared on Hollywood Squares many times
5. Won $32,000 on The $64,000 Question
6. Appeared on 1964's Shenanigans
7. Hosted Liar's Club
8. Appeared on Pantomime Quiz
9. Celebrity guests on You Don't Say
10. Appeared on Who's There? with Boris Karloff
11. Was the host on Your Lucky Clue (CBS 1952)

A) Vincent Price
B) Boris Karloff
C) Lisa Loring & Ken Weatherwax
D) Rod Serling
E) Boris Karloff
F) Tor Johnson
G) Carolyn Jones and John Astin
H) Vincent Price
I) Arlene Francis
J) Boris Karloff
K) Basil Rathbone

Answers page 140

Rod Serling, host of _____

Ghosts
Match each ghostly story with its film title

1. American students help a ghost find his missing head in an English castle
2. 1953 film about a haunted yacht
3. Two ghosts haunt a house on the Cornish coast
4. A group of old men share a dark secret about a ghostly woman
5. A widow falls in love with the spirit of a dead sea captain
6. Terry O'Quinn is haunted by a ghostly woman who thinks he is her long-lost lover
7. A 10-year-old helps the spirit of a young girl reunite with her ghostly mother
8. A doctor seeks to dispose of three spirits who haunt his house in this 1947 British film
9. A governess tutors two children who are menaced by the ghosts of their former governess and valet
10. A family inherits a house full of ghosts
11. An anthropologist and a selected group stay in a New England mansion to investigate paranormal occurrences
12. A timid typesetter has a chance to become a reporter if he can spend the night in a haunted house
13. An artist falls in love with a mysterious woman who he discovers died many years before
14. A Righteous Brothers song becomes a link between a ghostly husband and wife
15. Who are Peter Venkman, Ray Stantz and Egon Spengler?

A) Ghost Story
B) The Forgotten One
C) The Ghost of Rashemon Hall
D) The Uninvited
E) 13 Ghosts
F) The Headless Ghost
G) The Ghost and Mr. Chicken
H) The Ghost and Mrs. Muir
I) The Innocents
J) Ghost Ship
K) Portrait of Jennie
L) Ghostbusters
M) Lady in White
N) The Haunting
O) Ghost

Answers page 140

Ghouls Just Want To Have Fun
Match each actress and film with the monstrous temptress she portrayed

1. Susan Cabot (The Wasp Woman)
2. Gloria Talbott (Daughter of Dr. Jekyll)
3. Simone Simon (Cat People)
4. Colleen Gray (The Leech Woman)
5. Kathleen Burke (Island of Lost Souls)
6. Sandra Harrison (Blood of Dracula)
7. Allison Hayes (Attack of the 50 Foot Woman)
8. Marla English (The She Creature)
9. Sandra Knight (Frankenstein's Daughter)
10. Laurie Mitchell (Queen of Outer Space)
11. Faith Domergue (Cult of the Cobra)
12. Florence Marley (Queen of Blood)
13. Patricia Laffan (Devil Girl from Mars)
14. Lara Parker (Night of Dark Shadows)
15. Olga Baclanova (Freaks)
16. Mari Blanchard (She Devil)
17. Barbara Shelley (The Gorgon)
18. Gloria Holden (Dracula's Daughter)

A) Velana
B) Naya
C) Nancy Archer
D) Yllana
E) Janice Starlin
F) Cleopatra
G) Janet Smith
H) Carla
I) Angelique
J) Irena Dubrovna
K) Lota
L) Nancy Perkins
M) Trudy Morton
N) Lisa
O) Andrea Talbott
P) Marya Zaleska
Q) Kyra Zalis
R) June Talbot

Answers page 140

Godzilla and Friends

See how many questions you can answer concerning Toho's favorite giant lizard and his infamous friends

1. In what 1985 Tim Burton film would you see Godzilla battling Ghidrah on a soundstage?
2. Name the rock group that had a song entitled Godzilla
3. In what film would you find Godzilla fighting a giant lobster?
4. Name the 1959 American film title that featured Godzilla combating Angilus (an Ankylosaurus); for an extra bonus, what is significant about Godzilla's appearance in this film?
5. Name the 1957 film where miners find large insect larvae in a mine
6. Name the 1964 film that featured Godzilla as a hero for the first time
7. Name the original American release title for Godzilla vs. Mechagodzilla
8. What's the name of the natives' island protector who appears from a mountain to do battle with Mechagodzilla in Godzilla vs. Mechagodzilla?
9. What 1963 film featured Godzilla's first appearance in color?
10. Name the film where female aliens named the Kilaaks are controlling Godzilla and several other monsters
11. Name the Godzilla film that starred Nick Adams. As an extra bonus, can you name the other Japanese film in which he appeared?
12. In what film does a giant spider named Aspiga attack Godzilla's son?
13. What is Godzilla's son's name?
14. What actor from Godzilla King of the Monsters reprised his role in Godzilla 1985?
15. For what Godzilla film would you find a promo saying "Size Does Matter"?
16. Name the film where two tiny priestesses who are kidnapped and exploited by a sinister businessman and then are rescued by a giant caterpillar god

Answers page 132

Great Special Effects

When budgets for a B-monster film were low, the producers and directors would improvise with anything that could be utilized as a prop. These are just a few of those great special effects. Match the special effects with the movie title.

1. A postcard is used as a building in Chicago
2. Soap suds are used for fungus
3. A bubble-blower is a communication device
4. A mad scientist's disposal of body parts is a toilet flush
5. Windup Ladybug toys with pieces of fur coats and pipe cleaners made the monsters
6. A finger puppet is used for an alien
7. A shower curtain is used for a doorway covering in an airplane
8. A cloud effect is used with a piece of cotton wool stuck on a photograph
9. A balloon is used for the monster
10. A covering for a mangled victim looks like a toilet seat
11. Dogs are used with shaggy coats and fanged masks
12. A rubbery creature is pulled with strings
13. Pup tents or trash bags were used for the monsters
14. A director's fist was used as a shadowy creature

Answers page 140

A) The Brain Eaters
B) Frankenstein 1970
C) The Tingler
D) The Alligator People
E) The Killer Shrews
F) Attack of the Giant Leeches
G) The Crawling Eye
H) The Brain from Planet Arous
I) Robot Monster
J) Plan Nine from Outer Space
K) The Unknown Terror
L) Beast with a Million Eyes
M) Beginning of the End
N) Cat People

Halloween Haunts
Match each film title with its descriptive plot

1. Aliens land on Earth on Halloween and are mistaken for trick-or-treaters
2. At Halloween teens use an incantation to resurrect a witch and dead town residents
3. Two teenagers must spend the night in Dr. Frankenstein's castle on Halloween night
4. Kids sneak into a drive-in on Halloween to watch Night of the Living Dead
5. Bela Lugosi frightens trick-or-treaters at his home
6. The She Creature haunts a Halloween party
7. A thundering steed and its companion haunt the residents of Tarrytown
8. Teenage pranks on Halloween night make one teenager a little unnerved
9. An all-girls school scavenger hunt leads to murder on Halloween
10. Frankenstein & friends must convince a witch to fly over the moon on Halloween
11. Three children help their witch Grandma defeat an evil warlock
12. A family fortune is threatened by a gang of thieving electronic wizards
13. A babysitter is pursued by an escaped lunatic on Halloween
14. Four children learn the history of Halloween
15. Jack Skellington and friends celebrate a new holiday
16. A garbage man tries to find children who have disappeared on Halloween
17. The Olsen twins help a lady trapped in a mirror by an evil witch
18. Dr. Bobo the Magnificent entertains children with a magic act for a Halloween party

Answers page 141

A) Ed Wood
B) Frankenstein Sings
C) The Ghost of Dragstrip Hollow
D) Ernest Scared Stupid
E) The Midnight Hour
F) Frankenstein and Me
G) The Adventures of Icabod and Mr. Toad
H) Spaced Invaders
I) I Was a Teenage Werewolf
J) Halloween with the Addams Family
K) Blood of Dracula
L) The Halloween Tree
M) The Halloween that Almost Wasn't
N) Halloween Town
O) Halloween
P) The Nightmare Before Christmas
Q) Double Double Toil and Trouble
R) Curse of the Demon

Horrible Headlines

Extra, Extra read all about it. Match these newspaper headlines with the film that they were shown in.

1. The Daily Globe: Monster Takes Two
2. Transcript Journal: Back Breaker Claims Second Victim
3. Chicago Daily Register: Flying Death Strikes Again at Heathville
4. Police Baffled By Mysterious Theft of Altar Victims
5. Extra Hollywood Gazette: Beast Kills Man and Wife
6. The Ventura Post: Homicidal Maniac at Large
7. Arrest Near in Zoomer Murder, Murderer Caught by the Camera
8. The London Dispatch: Mysterious Goose Lane Murder, Unidentified Girl Horribly Mangled
9. Space Suits for First Moon Landings Unveiled
10. Hollywood Star Gazette: Is Surf Killer Maniac or Monster?
11. Los Angeles Chronicle: Doctor Killer Flees
12. Daily Local News: Local Bank is Robbed of $50,000
13. Wolfman Cured! Wins Surfing Contest
14. Mirror News: Weird Killer Still at Large
15. Washington Chronicle: Man from Mars Escapes
16. Huntington Park News: Crazed Man Kills Young Woman
17. Rockdale Daily News: Teenager in Mystery Death
18. The Daily Tribune: Sea Monster Kills Girl
19. Rachel Courier Express: Luther Hegg's Eerie Experience in Simmons Mansion
20. Hollywood Chronicle: Saucers Seen Over Hollywood

Answers page 141

A) Werewolf of London
B) The Corpse Vanishes
C) Homicidal
D) The Brute Man
E) Bride of the Monster
F) The Crawling Hand
G) The Horror of Party Beach
H) The Hideous Sun Demon
I) The Beach Girls and the Monster
J) Abbott and Costello Meet the Mummy
K) The Devil Bat
L) X the Man with the X-Ray Eyes
M) 4-D Man
N) I Was a Teenage Frankenstein
O) Transylvania 6-5000
P) I Was a Teenage Werewolf
Q) Beast of Yucca Flats
R) The Day the Earth Stood Still
S) The Ghost and Mr. Chicken
T) Plan Nine from Outer Space

Horrific Commercials

1. Footage from the Bride of Frankenstein was used for what General Mills cereal?
2. King Kong was used in an animated commercial for what car company?
3. In what commercial would you find Boris Karloff saying "experiment with it"?
4. In what commercial featuring Godzilla would you hear this phrase "Uh oh! I think I need a bigger box"!
5. In this commercial Boris used a torture test. Can you name it?
6. What horror film star did a commercial for Speidel watches?
7. Jerry Lacy (Reverend Trask) and Marie Wallace (Eve), both of Dark Shadows fame, appeared together in what deodorant commercial?
8. In this commercial the Count leaves his impression on what chocolate candy?
9. In the William Castle film Strait-Jacket, product placement is used for what popular soft drink?
10. What Hostess product is used with Dracula saying "Hey where's the cream filling?"
11. What literary monster tells us "Nothing works like Alka Seltzer Plus to get rid of the uglies"?
12. The Frankenstein monster is called Igor in this commercial as he searches the supermarket for what orange soda beverage?
13. What company known for their dessert treats was a sponsor for the 1966 Peanuts classic It's The Great Pumpkin Charlie Brown?
14. What character actor known for starring in some horror films did a commercial for Prudential Insurance?
15. What General Mills cereal did The Munsters do a commercial for?
16. What Universal monster does a commercial for Osteo Bi-Flex by Rexall?
17. Name the horror actor who did ads for Milton Bradley's Hangman and an Apple Sculpture Shrunken Head Kit.
18. What monster was used in a 1992 Nike commercial against superstar Charles Barkley, NBA champion?

Answers page 132-133

Monsters and horror stars do their bit for Madison Ave., including a Pepsi campaign in the 1990s.

Horror Actors' Last Roles
Match each actor with one of his last screen roles*

1. Autopsy of a Ghost
2. The Unholy Three
3. The Black Sleep
4. The Heart of Justice
5. Dracula vs. Frankenstein
6. Biggles
7. The Fear Chamber
8. The Patsy
9. The Beast of Yucca Flats
10. The Greatest Story Ever Told
11. Lost City of the Jungle
12. Buried Alive
13. Dracula vs. Frankenstein
14. Dangerous Blondes
15. David and Bathsheba
16. Last Train from Gun Hill
17. The Pumpkin Eater

A) Boris Karloff
B) Vincent Price
C) Claude Rains
D) John Carradine
E) Peter Cushing
F) Bela Lugosi
G) Lon Chaney, Sr.
H) Lon Chaney, Jr.
I) Peter Lorre
J) Basil Rathbone
K) Tor Johnson
L) Lionel Atwill
M) J. Carrol Naish
N) Dwight Frye
O) Sir Cedric Hardwicke
P) Glenn Strange
Q) George Zucco

Answers page 141

*Sources vary on some titles, so try to choose the film that is the closest to the date of the actor's death.

52   The 'Way-Out, Wonderful World

How To Become A Monster
Match each film title with its monster's origin

1. Special nutrients cause its gigantic growth
2. A plutonium bomb causes his problem
3. Radiation contaminates a sea creature
4. An atomic explosion awakens this Rhedosaur
5. A scientist brings a murderer back to life using electricity
6. A machine turns a scientist's thoughts to energy and into physical forms
7. A serum from fruit flies cures a woman with TB, but with criminal side effects
8. A couple experiment on natives using a fungus that creates monstrous creatures
9. A giant alien alters a woman's genetic balance
10. Radiation from an atomic plant and exposure to the sun causes the problem
11. An electric mechanism allows a man to penetrate solid matter
12. A matter-transmitting machine turns a man into an electrically charged monster
13. A serum turns tiny mammals into wolfish flesh eaters
14. Atomic radiation in the desert creates these giant creatures
15. A youth formula is made from the pineal gland of a living man mixed with a jungle powder
16. An enzyme-producing plant enlarges a chimpanzee

Answers page 141

A) Attack of the 50 Foot Woman
B) The 4-D Man
C) The Hideous Sun Demon
D) Them
E) The Leech Woman
F) She Devil
G) The Killer Shrews
H) The Projected Man
I) Fiend Without A Face
J) Konga
K) It Came from Beneath the Sea
L) Beginning of the End
M) The Amazing Colossal Man
N) Indestructible Man
O) The Unknown Terror
P) The Beast from 20,000 Fathoms

of Horror, Fantasy and Sci-Fi Movie Trivia

How To Destroy A Monster
Match the devices of death with the correct monster titles

1. Get shot with a radioactive isotope
2. Strike the Fissure of Orlando
3. Drive them into a lake with supersonic sound waves
4. Use a hot rod loaded with nitroglycerin
5. Let Clint Eastwood do it
6. Use a bazooka
7. Sink in a swamp of quicksand
8. Get stoned literally
9. Break its anti-matter shield with a Mumeson projector and shoot it
10. Use car headlights
11. Get knocked into a vat of hot wax
12. Throw carbolic acid at it and push it out a window with a chair
13. Get shot and stuck in a wall
14. Use 3RG toxic gas in a tunnel
15. Get the monster between two poles of electricity and make it fall on a stalagmite
16. Use a boulder, lightning and an octopus with atomic energy
17. Get shot with an electrified harpoon
18. Use a blowtorch in the eye
19. Get an atomic torpedo
20. Use a homemade acid bomb
21. Have the RAF drop firebombs
22. Get cut and bleed to death
23. Use a device to remove oxygen
24. Get electrocuted with high-tension wires in a dark corridor
25. Get an erupting volcano

A) Invasion of the Saucer Men
B) The Giant Claw
C) The Wasp Woman
D) House of Wax
E) 4-D Man
F) The Crawling Eye
G) Queen of Blood
H) It Conquered the World
I) Monster From Green Hell
J) Godzilla King of the Monsters
K) The Giant Gila Monster
L) The Fly
M) It Came from Beneath the Sea
N) The Thing from Another World
O) The Beginning of the End
P) Tarantula
Q) Earth vs. The Spider
R) The Brain from Planet Arous
S) The Black Scorpion
T) The Beast from 20,000 Fathoms
U) Bride of the Monster
V) The Amazing Colossal Man
W) The Alligator People
X) The Astounding She Monster
Y) The Deadly Mantis

Answers page 141

I Wore A Monster Costume

Match the film/TV title with the actor who wore a creature costume

1. Charlie Gemora
2. Lock Martin
3. Bob May
4. Ray "Crash" Corrigan
5. Regis Parton
6. Dick Sands
7. George Barrows
8. Dickie Owen
9. Pete Dunn
10. Robin Boston Barron
11. Ron Burke
12. Wade Popwell
13. Bob Bryant
14. Steven Ritch
15. Guy Buccola
16. Mike Lane

A) Zaat
B) The Day the Earth Stood Still
C) Destination Inner Space
D) War of the Worlds
E) Curse of the Faceless Man
F) Curse of the Mummy's Tomb
G) The Horror of Party Beach
H) Monster of Piedras Blancas
I) This Island Earth
J) Robot Monster
K) It The Terror from Beyond Space
L) Lost in Space (Robot)
M) Phantom from Space
N) Outer Limits (Keeper of the Purple Twilight as Ikar)
O) Attack of the Giant Leeches
P) The Werewolf

Answers page 141

Invisibly Transparent

1. In what film is he known as The Invisible One?
2. Who was originally offered the role of The Invisible Man?
3. Who starred as the invisible man in the second entry of the series?
4. Name the actress who stars in the 1940 Universal film The Invisible Woman
5. Name the actor who played the invisible man in Invisible Agent and The Invisible Man's Revenge
6. Name the John Carpenter film about a governmental experiment that turns an average working man into an invisible man
7. In what film would you find an invisible man wearing a fez and sounding like Sydney Greenstreet?
8. In what film does a boxer framed for murder become invisible to search for the real killer?
9. Name the film involving an invisible bank robber played by Douglas Kennedy
10. What 1950 Republic serial had The Phantom Ruler using a chemically treated cloak and a beam of light to become invisible?

Answers page 133

It Landed on the Cutting Room Floor

In some cases, film scenes were deleted and landed on the cutting room floor, often due to horrific content, budgetary reasons or continuity. Can you match each deleted scene with its film title?

1. A bubbling swamp with large vampire bats
2. Lon Chaney, Jr. wrestles a bear
3. A spider pit with a giant spider
4. A woman is shown her many past lives
5. A monster kills a burgomaster
6. A giant devilfish battles a giant monster
7. Ross Elliot portrays a lawyer killed in a jail cell
8. A head is shown in a birdcage
9. An opening prologue where a sane woman is attacked by lunatics
10. A final curtain speech saying "There are such things."
11. Prologue with subject concerning the five senses
12. A decapitated head is held on by means of straps and iron braces
13. An inquisition about a bullet wound
14. A recorded will is played and the voice sounds like John Carradine

A) The Pit and the Pendulum
B) I Was a Teenage Frankenstein
C) Tarzan Escapes
D) King Kong
E) Frankenstein Conquers the World
F) The Wolfman
G) X The Man with the X-Ray Eyes
H) The Mummy (1932)
I) Indestructible Man
J) Mark of the Vampire
K) Bride of Frankenstein
L) Mad Love
M) Dracula
N) Young Frankenstein

Answers page 141

The 'Way-Out, Wonderful World

Jekyll and Hyde
Match each actor with his film version

1. This version relied on expression rather than makeup
2. 1990 film version with Cheryl Ladd
3. An Irish maid is employed by Dr. Jekyll
4. 1920 silent film version
5. Keeping Jekyll and Hyde in the family
6. Gloria Talbot is framed
7. Won an Oscar for best actor
8. The mention of various foods causes transformation
9. Night Gallery episode "With Apologies to Dr. Jekyll"
10. Hammer Hyde
11. Doctor tries to turn ward's suitor into a monster
12. Professor Kelp/Buddy Love
13. Film star of I Monster
14. Dan Curtis TV production
15. Unauthorized adaptation Der Januskopf
16. 1973 TV Musical

A) Boris Karloff
B) Frederic March
C) John Barrymore
D) Jerry Lewis
E) Jack Palance
F) Conrad Veidt
G) Adam West
H) Louis Hayward
I) Spencer Tracy
J) Arthur Shields
K) Michael Caine
L) Bob Denver
M) John Malkovich
N) Paul Massie
O) Christopher Lee
P) Kirk Douglas

Answers page 141

John Agar

Fans will always remember this talented actor who co-starred with the legendary John Wayne in three of his pictures. Monster fans, however, will remember him in the genre with his battle against Mole People, a giant tarantula and the Gillman. Match each film role along with its film title in which John Agar starred.

1. John plays a scientist at a Florida oceanarium
2. He's a army major using military tactics on alien visitors
3. An Arizona doctor attempts to solve a case of acromegaly
4. An archaeologist discovers an underground civilization
5. John's a physicist possessed by an evil alien
6. A chemist exposed to a deadly gas
7. John stars as a New York City mayor in this film
8. An astronaut has his mind controlled by a huge cellular brain
9. John has a cameo in a Clive Barker film
10. John is a geologist in the Florida Everglades
11. John stars as Dr. Farrell with Wendell Corey
12. John is placed in a glass tube
13. An expedition encounters a mutant in this 1968 Larry Buchanan film
14. John helps his fiancée solve the mystery behind the full moon murders
15. 1988 sci-fi film involving a nuclear holocaust
16. 1951 fantasy with Lucille Ball
17. Agar opposes an alien visitor who can control his mind
18. A ray gun when fired causes people to tell the truth

A) Curse of the Swamp Creature
B) King Kong (1976)
C) Attack of the Puppet People
D) The Magic Carpet
E) Revenge of the Creature
F) Miracle Mile
G) The Mole People
H) Daughter of Dr. Jekyll
I) Zontar the Thing from Venus
J) The Brain from Planet Arous
K) Invisible Invaders
L) Journey to the Seventh Planet
M) Tarantula
N) Night Fright
O) The Rocket Man
P) Hand of Death
Q) Night Breed
R) Women of the Prehistoric Planet

Answers page 141

Jungle Madness

1. Allison Hayes attempts to kill her husband with a voodoo doll in this 1957 film
2. On a tropical island Dr. Zabor turns a young man into a gorilla
3. Features Paula the Ape Woman in her second sequel
4. A murdered native comes to life as a tree monster
5. A love-struck ape kidnaps a woman on an African safari
6. Lou Costello meets a giant ape
7. Jungle Jim film involving natives and space aliens

Answers page 133

Just Mad About Karloff

Match each mad doctor film starring Boris Karloff with its correct profile

1. An inventor bent on helping the war effort
2. London doctor with a dual personality
3. A doctor develops a process for switching minds
4. A scientist develops a weapon aliens want
5. An escaped mad scientist with a traveling horror show
6. A surgeon becomes addicted to his anesthetic
7. A mad doctor extracts spinal fluid from his victims
8. A doctor invents a mechanical heart device, which brings him back from the dead
9. A scientist and his living rock
10. A medieval doctor helps a nobleman escape from an evil count
11. Mad doctor uses TV crew as spare parts
12. Gem gives professor eternal life
13. Doctor invents serum to prevent aging but uses criminal blood in the serum
14. A doctor uses poison for money to help in furthering his research
15. A doctor develops suspended animation
16. An inventor's burglar alarm is stolen
17. A hypnotist develops a device to control people
18. A doctor traces brain waves from the dead
19. Scientist contaminated by radioactivity
20. A doctor does brain transplant on dying friend with a gangster's brain
21. A political scientist is being controlled by an enemy agent

Answers page 141

A) The Man They Could Not Hang
B) House of Frankenstein
C) Before I Hang
D) Black Friday
E) The Man With Nine Lives
F) The Invisible Ray
G) The Man Who Lived Again
H) The Ape
I) Frankenstein 1970
J) The Devil Commands
K) The Boogie Man Will Get You
L) Abbott and Costello Meet Dr. Jekyll and Mr. Hyde
M) The Incredible Invasion
N) Corridors of Blood
O) The Fear Chamber
P) The Black Castle
Q) The Ghoul
R) Juggernaut
S) Night Key
T) The Sorcerers
U) The Venetian Affair

Literally Speaking
Match the genre film with the story it was based on.
As an extra bonus match its author

1. Who Goes There?
2. The Foghorn
3. I Am Legend
4. The Adaptive Ultimate
5. The Thought Monster
6. The Cosmic Frame
7. Seven Keys to Baldpate
8. The Horla
9. Farewell to the Master
10. Dracula's Guest
11. Uneasy Freehold
12. Benighted
13. Career of A Comet
14. Black Alibi
15. None Came Back
16. A Taste for Honey

A) Invasion of the Saucer Men
B) Fiend Without A Face
C) House of the Long Shadows
D) The Day the Earth Stood Still
E) She Devil
F) Dracula's Daughter
G) Valley of the Dragons
H) Diary of a Madman
I) The Thing from Another World
J) The Deadly Bees
K) The Uninvited
L) Rocketship XM
M) The Beast from 20,000 Fathoms
N) The Old Dark House
O) The Leopard Man
P) The Omega Man

A1) Ray Bradbury
B2) John Campbell, Jr.
C3) H.F. Heard
D4) Paul Fairman
E5) Cornell Woolrich
F6) Richard Matheson
G7) Jules Verne
H8) Amelia Reynolds Long
I9) Stanley G. Weinbaum
J10) Curt Neumann
K11) Bram Stoker
L12) Earl Derr Biggers
M13) Guy De Maupassant
N14) Harry Bates
O15) Dorothy Macardle
P16) J.B. Priestley

Answers page 142

Made For TV Sci-Fi/Horror/Fantasy
Match each profile with its made for TV film

1. Mary Shelley's novel starring Leonard Whiting
2. Dennis Weaver suspects there's a vampire in New York
3. Bradford Dillman is a werewolf in the Louisiana bayou
4. Zombies are found in 1930s Chicago
5. A reporter investigates vampire killings in Las Vegas
6. Gale Sondergaard commits murder for an amulet
7. Stephen King Nosferatu-like vampire
8. In Seattle a 100-year-old crazed killer seeks blood for a fountain of youth serum
9. Policeman (Ernest Borgnine's) partner is a robot
10. 1977 Dan Curtis production with full moon murders and a mysterious woman
11. A big-game hunter poses as a werewolf
12. A scientist and his son discover a mutated lizard
13. A Victorian bed and breakfast inn is haunted by an evil ghost
14. Cathy Lee Crosby's 1974 film
15. TV movie that was also shown theatrically
16. Los Angeles vampire detective
17. TV movie starring Donna Mills based on a 1975 film

Answers page 142

A) The Cat Creature
B) The Dead Don't Die
C) Scream of the Wolf
D) The Night Strangler
E) Future Cop
F) The Night Stalker
G) Wonder Woman
H) Frankenstein the True Story
I) Salem's Lot
J) Duel
K) Moon of the Wolf
L) McCloud Meets Dracula
M) Curse of the Black Widow
N) Gargantua
O) The Haunting of Seacliff Inn
P) Nick Knight
Q) The Stepford Husbands

A Magic Moment
Match each film title with its magical profile

1. An evil sorcerer kidnaps a princess then tries to feed her to his dragon on her 18th birthday
2. A stage illusionist's assistant murders his employer and assumes his identity
3. Bela Lugosi portrays evil scientist Roxor
4. An insane stage illusionist fakes his own death to correct a disastrous mistake
5. An evil magician kidnaps Princess Elaine with Kerwin Matthews in hot pursuit
6. A George Pal production starring Tony Curtis
7. 1978 film with Anthony Hopkins
8. 1973 TV program with Bill Bixby
9. John, George, Paul and Ringo starred in this film
10. 1944 Charlie Chan mystery reissued as Meeting at Midnight
11. 1951 Sam Katzman adventure/fantasy film

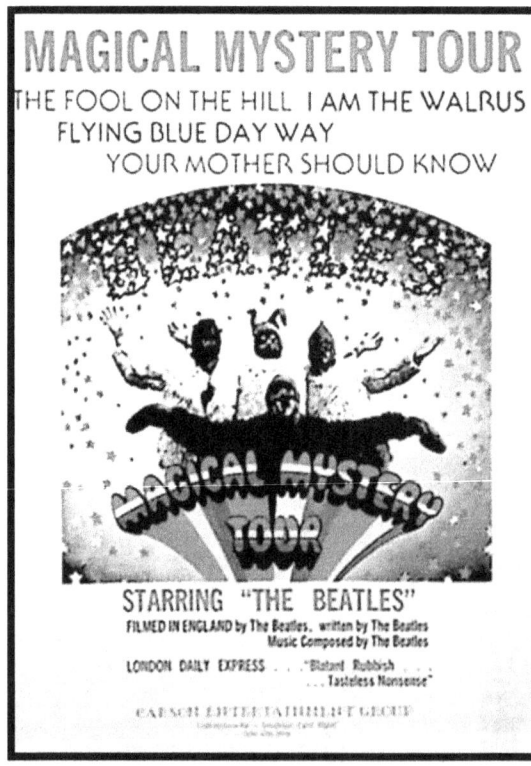

A) The Magic Carpet
B) Houdini
C) The Magic Sword
D) Magic
E) Black Magic
F) Magical Mystery Tour
G) The Mad Magician
H) Two on a Guillotine
I) Jack the Giant Killer
J) The Magician
K) Chandu the Magician

Answers page 142

Monster Ad Campaign
Match each poster ad campaign phrase with its movie title

1. Body of a Boy! Mind of a Monster! Soul of an Unearthly Thing!
2. Crawling Slimy Things Terror Bent on Destroying the World
3. The Flowers that Kill in the Spring
4. When the Screen Screams You'll Scream Too, if You Value Your Life
5. Once it was Human Even as You and I
6. The Monster Demands a Mate
7. The Fantastic Night of Terror that Menaced the Fate of the World
8. He Begins Where Dracula Left Off
9. New Horrors! Mad Science Spawns Evil Fiends
10. How Did It Get Here?
11. The Grave Can't Hold It, Nothing Human Can Stop It!
12. Moon Monsters Launch Attack Against Earth
13. It Came from Another World
14. Centuries of Passion Pent Up in his Savage Heart!
15. You'll Know When They Prowl for the Master Monster of Them All
16. Bullets Won't Kill It! Flames Can't Hurt It! Nothing Can Stop It!
17. Terror Comes in Small Packages
18. Like Nothing You've Ever Seen Before
19. The Weirdest Visitor the Earth Has Ever Seen
20. Never Before so Much Wickedness Under One Roof
21. A Creature from Beyond the Stars—Evil, Beautiful, Deadly
22. Invisible Atom Horror! Here to Spy on Earth
23. What was the Unspeakable Secret of the Sea of Lost Ships?

Answers page 142

A) Blood of the Vampire
B) Creature from the Black Lagoon
C) The Fly
D) The Brain Eaters
E) Giant from the Unknown
F) The Thing from Another World
G) Abbott & Costello Meet Dr. Jekyll and Mr. Hyde
H) The Man from Planet X
I) Fiend without a Face
J) The Thing That Couldn't Die
K) Attack of the Puppet People
L) Bride of Frankenstein
M) Earth vs. the Spider
N) I Was a Teenage Frankenstein
O) Gorgo
P) Devil Girl From Mars
Q) House of Frankenstein
R) Little Shop of Horrors
S) Robot Monster
T) The Tingler
U) The Astounding She Monster
V) The Cosmic Man
W) Creature from the Haunted Sea

of Horror, Fantasy and Sci-Fi Movie Trivia

Monster Anagrams

Unscramble the following anagrams to discover the film title/location
(ignore the punctuation)

1. Four? O, such a deal   clue: 1945 monster rally

2. Neat! They hurl   clue: 1957 John Carradine sci-fi

3. hot cig   clue: Ken Russell film

4. Lee, stab Tom   clue: location, 1960

5. That darn name: Helen   clue: 1953 sci-fi goes prehistoric

6. Thin red rum oozes   clue: 1933 Lionel Atwill chiller

7. I spy Debra B.   clue: "maddest story ever told"

8. He meant pa   clue: Bela monkeys around

9. Such a rose harp!   clue: blood-sucking mummy

10. We both abler be   clue: 1972 defrosted sequel

Answers page 133

Thanks to Anthony Ambrogio working on the anagrams to make them a tribute to the FM days

Monster Anthologies
Match each anthology film with one of its stories

1. A missing horror star
2. A disembodied hand haunts its would-be murderer
3. A haunted mirror
4. A St. Valentine's Day greeting is given from the grave
5. Husband and wife disagree about a hungry tree
6. A hypnotist keeps a dying man alive
7. A Zuni doll comes alive
8. A starving artist falls in love with a gargoyle
9. Two friends bring an old love back to life with rejuvenating water
10. A man becomes a menu item at a restaurant for vampires
11. A movie director has a hard time leaving a village of Humgoos
12. A doctor, medical students and electricity bring an insane killer back to life
13. Several limbs seek revenge on an unfaithful husband and his girlfriend
14. A murderer is haunted by a sinister image on a painting
15. A young boy by sheer will makes things appear
16. A centuries-old Arctic creature is still alive
17. One segment includes a parody on The Invisible Man
18. Peter Cushing's character keeps Edgar Allan Poe alive

A) Dr. Terror's House of Horrors
B) Tales from the Crypt
C) Vault of Horror
D) Trilogy of Terror
E) Tales of Terror
F) The House that Dripped Blood
G) Dead of Night
H) Tales that Witness Madness
I) Dr. Terror's Gallery of Horrors
J) Tales from the Darkside: The Movie
K) Twice Told Tales
L) Asylum
M) The Monster Club
N) Night Gallery
O) Creepshow
P) Amazon Women on the Moon
Q) Twilight Zone: The Movie
R) Torture Garden

Answers page 142

Monster Beach Party

1. In what AIP beach film would you find Boris Karloff as an art collector?
2. What horror actor portrayed the strongest man in the world in Muscle Beach Party?
3. What horror actor has a cameo in the first beach film, Beach Party?
4. What other actor known for being in some horror films was in The Ghost in the Invisible Bikini with Boris Karloff?
5. Frank Sinatra, Jr. wrote the music score for what beach monster film?
6. Marta Kristen (Judy Robinson of Lost in Space fame) portrays a mermaid in this AIP beach film. What is its title?
7. Radioactive sea monsters crash a pajama party and a local beach. Can you name the film?
8. Name the film where a live disembodied hand is found on a beach
9. Name the film where two teenagers go for a swim at the beach and are attacked by giant mollusks
10. Name the actress who was married to Jim Nicholson (AIP studio mogul) who plays The Ghost in the Invisible Bikini
11. Name the film where a lighthouse-keeper's daughter is pursued by a sea monster
12. What 1975 film spawned many sequels, one of which was in 3-D?
13. In what AIP beach film would you find actress Elizabeth Montgomery (of TV's Bewitched fame) as a witch doctor's daughter?

Answers page 133

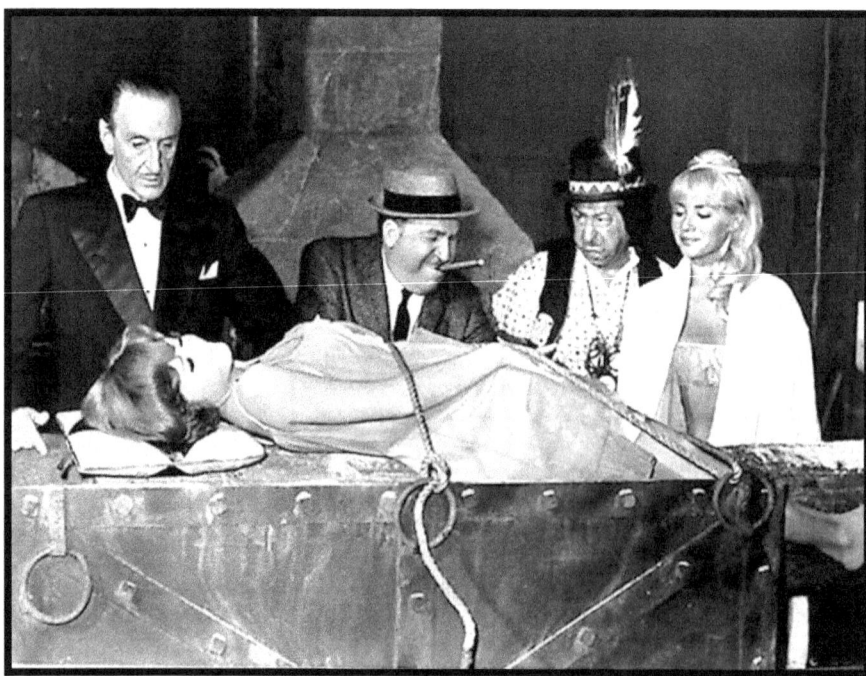

The 'Way-Out, Wonderful World

Monster Character Traits

Match each monstrous character trait with its film title

1. Flying brains with antennas
2. Extraterrestrial carrot man
3. Giant plutonium-blasted man
4. An amphibious missing link
5. Furry king
6. Radioactive giant crustaceans
7. Giant caterpillar like slugs
8. Stowaway Martian
9. Extraterrestrial rocks
10. Cannibalistic underground creatures
11. Prehistoric baby dinosaur
12. Giant cube-shaped robot
13. A one-eyed octopus
14. Giant bird from outer space
15. Giant lobster called a Gargon
16. A crawling carpet
17. A bat-rat spider Martian
18. Martian in an ape suit

A) The Monolith Monsters
B) The Time Machine
C) Monster from the Ocean Floor
D) Attack of the Crab Monsters
E) Gorgo
F) The Monster that Challenged the World
G) The Thing from Another World
H) Teenagers from Outer Space
I) It! The Terror from Beyond Space
J) The Amazing Colossal Man
K) Kronos
L) The Creature from the Black Lagoon
M) The Giant Claw
N) Fiend Without a Face
O) Robot Monster
P) King Kong
Q) The Angry Red Planet
R) The Creeping Terror

Answers page 142

of Horror, Fantasy and Sci-Fi Movie Trivia

Monster Film Stars Debut
Match each actor with his first film role

1. The Man on the Flying Trapeze
2. His Majesty the American
3. Corridor of Mirrors
4. The Man in the Iron Mask
5. M
6. Service De Luxe
7. The Dreyfus Case
8. Build Thy House
9. Eve's Daughter
10. The Leopard
11. Bird of Paradise
12. Poor Jake's Demise
13. The Night Bird
14. Bright Lights
15. Innocent
16. Double Cross Roads
17. Riches and Rogues
18. Wild Horse

A) Vincent Price
B) George Zucco
C) Claude Rains
D) Lionel Atwill
E) Tor Johnson
F) Boris Karloff
G) Bela Lugosi
H) Peter Cushing
I) Peter Lorre
J) Lon Chaney Sr.
K) Dwight Frye
L) Lon Chaney, Jr.
M) Christopher Lee
N) Glenn Strange
O) John Carradine
P) J. Carroll Naish
Q) Basil Rathbone
R) Sir Cedric Hardwicke

Answers page 142

Monster Movie Within A Movie

1. In Earth vs. the Spider, what film does Mike want to see at his father's movie theater?
2. In Attack of the Puppet People John Agar and June Kenney have a date at the drive-in. What AIP film is showing under the stars?
3. In the film Matinee, what is the name of the film that premieres at the Key West Strand theater?
4. In Terror in the Year 5000, what AIP film is on the marquee that Dr. Hedges and friends see?
5. In Beach Blanket Bingo, what AIP sci-fi film is on the television when Eric Von Zipper kidnaps Sugar Cane?
6. What Universal horror comedy is on the TV when David Bowie and Carl Perkins are in a deadly fight in Into the Night?
7. What 1980 horror film featured clips from The Wolfman?
8. In the film Gorgo, what Hammer film is on the marquee in Picadilly Circus?
9. In Bowery At Midnight, what Monogram picture with Bela Lugosi is seen on the marquee?
10. What Ray Harryhausen film is on TV in 1998's Godzilla?
11. In Halloween 2, what 1968 horror film is on TV?
12. What horror film is on the theater marquee in the 1973 movie American Graffiti. Hint: it was the producer's first picture as a director.
13. The Outer Limits episode "One Hundred Days of the Dragon" is seen on television in what 1993 Robin Williams film?
14. In what Jim Carrey film would you see a scene from The Day the Earth Stood Still?
15. In what 1958 sci-fi classic would teenagers in a theater be watching the movie Daughter of Horror?
16. In the film Great Balls of Fire, Dennis Quaid and Wynona Ryder are watching what sci-fi film on TV?
17. In the Joe Dante film Gremlins. what sci-fi movie do Billy and Gizmo have on TV when he mistakenly feeds the gremlins after midnight?
18. ET surfs the TV and views what 1955 Universal sci-fi film?
19. What sci-fi classic is shown on the TV in the film Eight-Legged Freaks?
20. What 1966 Jerry Lewis comedy featured clips from Frankenstein (1931)?
21. In the film Ferris Bueller's Day Off what Godzilla film is on the movie theater marquee?

Answers page 133

Monster Movie Quotes
Match the horror/sci-fi quote with its movie title

1. "To God there is no zero. I still exist."
2. "Gort, Klaatu barada nikto."
3. "He went for a little walk."
4. "Here we go gathering nuts in May."
5. "Keep watching the skies."
6. "Last night I saw a flying object that couldn't have possibly been from this planet, but I can't say a word. I'm muzzled by army brass."
7. "All I said was that he looked like Boris Karloff."
8. "Soon you will be as big as a giant or like all the others dead."
9. "You're crazy to know who I am, aren't you? All right I'll show you."
10. "There's no place in this civilization for a 60-foot man."
11. "And they used Bon Ami."
12. "What a delicious torture!"
13. "A most interesting cranium!"
14. "A white spider! That must be the ghost of the Black Widow."
15. "Tom Stewart killed me!"
16. "Only when we have to fight to stay human do we realize how precious it is."
17. "If there's much more like this. What you say pal? We give ourselves up and let 'em hang us."
18. "Go soak your fat head."
19. "When an armed and threatening powers land uninvited in our capital we don't meet it with tea and cookies."
20. "When stars are bright on a frosty night. Beware thy bane on the rocky lane."
21. "Basil Rathbone must be giving a party."

Answers page 142

A) Bride of the Monster
B) Plan Nine from Outer Space
C) War of the Colossal Beast
D) The Invisible Man
E) The Ghost and Mr. Chicken
F) The Raven (1935)
G) Invasion of the Body Snatchers
H) The Mummy (1932)
I) Bela Lugosi Meets a Brooklyn Gorilla
J) Arsenic and Old Lace
K) Spooks Run Wild
L) Tormented
M) Bride of Frankenstein
N) The Day the Earth Stood Still
O) The Incredible Shrinking Man
P) Attack of the Giant Leeches
Q) The Invisible Man
R) Earth vs. the Flying Saucers
S) The Thing from Another World
T) The Undying Monster
U) The Ghost Breakers

Monster Pop
Match each novelty song with its artist

1. The Lurch
2. Purple People Eater
3. Castin' My Spell On You
4. Witch Doctor
5. Haunted House
6. The Headless Horseman
7. The Addams Family
8. The Flying Saucers Pt. 1
9. Attack of the Killer Tomatoes
10. Monster Mash
11. Dinner with Drac
12. The Blob
13. The Thing
14. Werewolves of London
15. Monsters Holiday
16. This is Halloween
17. I Put A Spell on You
18. Witch Queen of New Orleans
19. Quentin's Theme
20. Slime Creatures from Outer Space
21. Ben
22. My Old Flame
23. Martian Hop
24. My Son The Vampire
25. The Purple People Eater Meets the Witch Doctor
26. Ghostbusters

A) Lewis Lee
B) Phil Harris
C) Lon Chaney, Jr.
D) The Five Blobs
E) Screamin' Jay Hawkins
F) Danny Elfman
G) Redbone
H) David Selby
I) Ted Cassidy
J) Johnny Otis
K) Sheb Wooley
L) Bing Crosby
M) Weird Al Yankovic
N) Bobby "Boris" Pickett
O) Warren Zevon
P) Vic Mizzy
Q) Jumpin' Gene Simmons
R) Michael Jackson
S) Ray Parker, Jr.
T) David Seville
U) John Zacherle
V) Joe South
W) The Randells
X) Spike Jones
Y) Buchanan and Goodman
Z) Allan Sherman

Answers page 142

Monstrous Props

Film sets and props were recycled over and over again for other pictures. See if you can answer the following questions...

1. In the film Experiment in Terror what 13 Ghosts prop can be seen in the bank office?
2. Spot, The Munsters pet is seen in what 1950s dinosaur film?
3. Forbidden Planet space suits were in what other space opera film?
4. Name the film where claws from The Mole People (from Universal Studios monster molds) were used
5. The giant spider from Catwomen in the Moon was used again in the remake. Can you name it?
6. Name the original film where the octopus used in Bride of the Monster supposedly came from
7. Tamara the eight-legged tarantula from Tarantula was used again in another Universal sci-fi film. Name the film.
8. The metal robot costume used on Captain Video originally appeared in a Gene Autry film. Name the film.
9. Roy Barcroft's uniform worn in The Purple Monster Strikes was used again in what 1952 serial involving moon men?
10. Where did Gorog, the robot from The Bowery Boys Meet the Monsters, make a cameo in a 1962 sci-fi film, which supposedly was Andy Warhol's favorite movie?
11. This film reused the sets from The Raven (1963). Name the film.
12. In what film starring Boris, Bela and Lorre is a Triceratops prop from the film King Kong shown that failed to make the final cut?
13. In what Universal horror classic was part of the grand hall in White Zombie used before?
14. What 1954 film with John Agar has Klaatu's spacesuit in it?
15. What Val Lewton film used the church building from The Bells of St.Mary's?
16. What film, directed by Frank R. Strayer in 1935, utilized the bell tower from Universal's The Hunchback of Notre Dame and the street from Bride of Frankenstein?

Answers page 134

Monster Star Quotes
Match the star with his/her actual quote

1. "So you've come to conquer the world!"
2. "It was actually a sectopus, not an octopus."
3. "Dracula is a blessing and a curse and Dracula never dies."
4. "My five-year-old daughter can write something better than that."
5. "That grinning, glowing, globular invader of your living room is an inhabitant of the pumpkin patch and if your door bell rings and nobody's there, that was no Martian, it's Halloween."
6. "I'll never quit the stage or the films. I'd go out of my skull!"
7. "The man who rescued me from the living dead and restored my soul."
8. "I don't want to go down in history as a monster. I've never played a frog that swallowed a city or something like that."
9. "I give epitaphs, not autographs!"
10. "I learn the lines and pray to God."
11. "Some people say Casablanca or Citizen Kane. I say: Jason and the Argonauts is the greatest film ever made."

A) Lou Costello
B) Peter Lorre
C) Beverly Garland
D) Bela Lugosi
E) Orson Welles
F) John Carradine
G) Boris Karloff (speaking about Val Lewton)
H) Ray Harryhausen
I) Maila Nurmi
J) Claude Rains
K) Tom Hanks

Answers page 142

Monster Toys

1. On an episode of The Munsters, name the toy that is mistaken for Herman's child
2. In the 1960s these bubble bath products featured the Wolfman, the Frankenstein monster, the Creature and the Mummy
3. Name the 1967 bubble gum cards set that featured AIP photos, a funny quote and "Did it ever happen?"stories on the back
4. In 1964 this talking hand puppet released by Mattel was based on a character from a horror TV sitcom
5. True or false: in 1979 Aladdin produced a line of lunch boxes and thermoses known as the Universal Movie Monsters
6. These 1963 Marx six-inch-high figures could be found at your five-and-dime store in orange and blue plastic. Can you name the six Universal monsters that were available?
7. Name the Milton Bradley board game where you wore fangs and constructed a skeleton
8. 1964 saw this giant model produced by Aurora
9. Name the 1960s Frankenstein toy whose pants fall down
10. This game glowed in the dark and featured black cats, creepy houses and ghosts
11. This 1962 card series featured bug-eyed aliens invading Earth
12. This 1960 toy resembled the giant from Jack the Giant Killer
13. Name the company that produced a line of children's Halloween costumes in 1963
14. In 1992 Bally introduced a pinball machine with what Universal monster?
15. In 1962 Milton Bradley produced this monster card game based on a classic children's card game
16. Name the candy dispenser toy that released a Universal monster line in the 1960s

Answers page 133

Monster Who Am I?
Guess who or what I am from the clues

1. An Allied Artist film; Based on the novel by Maurice Sandoz; Co-stars include Michael Pate and Hillary Brooke; Filmed in 3-D; Directed by William Cameron Menzies; A 1953 film; involves a 200-year-old creature; A Scottish ancestral home; Richard Carlson stars; The creature is a frog

2. An Associated Producers film; A 1959 film; Dan Seymour and David Frankham co-star; Directed by Edward L. Bernds; A funeral parlor is a scene for two murders; This was a sequel to a classic film; It also furthered another sequel in 1965; Vincent Price reprises his role

3. Born in the Bronx in 1928; Has appeared on TV in shows like Taxi and Wagon Train; Has been seen on the drive-in theater screen many times; Played Burson Fouch in Little Shop of Horrors; Has had cameo roles in several Joe Dante films; Satirically funny in films; His character hated Gremlins; Played a vacuum salesman in a movie; A Roger Corman alumni; He played Walter Paisley in A Bucket of Blood

4. Born in 1944; Her last name was Glazier; Played opposite Ralph Bates in a film; She co-starred with David Niven; Was directed by Terence Fisher; She co-starred with Peter Cushing; She was a tasty morsel for The Ghoul; Christopher Lee put the bite on her; A Hammer heroine; She played Anna Spangler in Frankenstein Must Be Destroyed

5. A 1939 film; Was directed by Rowland V Lee; Josephine Hutchinson co-starred; A fairy tale book is coveted; It was third in its series; A Universal picture; It was to be Universal's first Technicolor production; Atwill and Rathbone appeared in the film; This was Lugosi's second greatest role; This was Karloff's last performance as the Frankenstein Monster in a feature film

6. I'd been on two television shows when my movie was released; I've graced the cover of Fantastic Monsters of the Films; AIP is my favorite movie studio; My lunch hooks were in my film but never used; I'm closely associated with Bridey Murphy; Bob Burns knows me well; I've been altered several times; I've starred with Marla English twice; I preferred being called Cuddles; Paul Blaisdell was my closest friend

7. I was born in Monroe, Louisiana; In 1920 I was on Broadway; I was put on contract at Monogram Pictures; I was in A Haunting We Will Go with Laurel and Hardy; I've played several servant roles; I've been in zombie films for Monogram; I was on The Bill Cosby Show (1969-1971); I was an African American; I was in 15 Charlie Chan films; I was in Spider Baby with Lon Chaney, Jr.

8. I was born in 1916; The first imagi-film I saw was The Lost World; I appeared on TV in 1947; I received the first Hugo Award in 1953; My house's former owner was Jon Hall; I was a literary agent; I've had over 50 cameos in films; I collect monster memorabilia; I coined the phrase "Sci-Fi"; I was the editor of Famous Monsters of Filmland

9. I was born in Hawaii; I was a law school student; I starred in Nabonga; I was Captain Gallant on TV; I played Kaspa in King of the Jungle; I starred in a Fred Olen Ray film; I was Tarzan in a film; I was on TV with Gil Gerard; I was a former Olympic swimmer; I starred as Buck Rogers and Flash Gordon

10. I was born in 1913; I was a 20th Century Fox contract player; I was afraid of typecasting; I collaborated on a song with Milton Berle; I was in Blood and Sand with Tyrone Power; I used to say, "I was a descendant of John Wilkes Booth"; I was said to be gay; I had an obsession about weight; Vincent Price delivered my eulogy; I was the star of The Lodger

11. I was an RKO stock player; I played a medical student in The Body Snatcher; I worked on a Edgar Ulmer film; I was a director, producer and writer; My dog Egan played in a film with me under the same name; I had a small role in Dick Tracy Meets Gruesome; I was Dan the dog in the film Bedlam; I was in The Incredible Petrified World with John Carradine; I married Alyce King, a singer in the group The King Sisters; I was The Hideous Sun Demon

12. I was an usher at Vincent Price's first wedding; I played a dinner guest in a Rod Taylor film; I accompanied Cesare Romero on The Lost Continent; I was in the film Soylent Green; I was in two AIP films; Kevin McCarthy sought my help in a motion picture; I was in a 1950s Universal classic and got clawed; I was a General in a sci-fi cult TV series; I fed my fiancée to a crocodile; I turned Michael Landon into a werewolf

13. I was in a film called House of the Damned; I played Kolos in The Human Duplicators; I was in an Elvis Presley film; I played a Diablero and a bayou beast; I was on The Phantom Planet; I was in a Arch Hall, Jr. film; I was in "To Serve Man" (a Twilight Zone episode); I've been mistaken for Ted Cassidy; I was Eegah; I was Jaws in two James Bond films

14. I was in From the Earth to the Moon; Bela Lugosi and I were in The Phantom Creeps; I was in Dinosaur Island; I was with two teenagers in Earth vs. the Spider; Ro-Man and I were together in Robot Monster; I was destroyed in a volcano eruption in She Demons; I was camouflage bunker #6 in Invisible Invaders; The Quetzelcoatl exited me in The Flying Serpent; I was the domain on Earth for It Conquered the World

Answers page 134

Monstrous Bloopers
Can you match the films with its significant bloopers?

1. You can see a movable gravestone
2. A telephone pole along the Amazon River
3. A vampire's image is reflected in a mirror
4. A ragged piece of cardboard is left attached to a lamp
5. A cadaver on an operating table is wearing neatly polished shoes
6. Footprints in the snow look like shoeprints
7. A plant-eating dinosaur eats a man
8. A caveman shows his underwear while exiting a window
9. A man's legs can be seen lurching over rocks
10. A man's shoes are seen where there should be flippers

A) Return of the Ape Man
B) Destination Inner Space
C) Plan Nine from Outer Space
D) Frankenstein
E) Son of Dracula
F) Attack of the Crab Monsters
G) The Invisible Man
H) Dracula
I) King Kong
J) Creature from the Black Lagoon

Answers page 142

Monstrous Movie Songs
Match each unlikely song with its film title

1. The Zombie Stomp
2. Eeny-Meeny-Miney-Mo
3. The Cat Came Back
4. Stella by Starlight
5. Geronimo
6. The Ballad of San Sebastian
7. Puppy Love
8. You've Got To Have Ee-ooo
9. Papa-Ooo-Mow-Mow
10. It's the Mummy
11. Aurora
12. Special Date
13. The Old Rock House on the Brownsville Road
14. Mixed Up Zombie Stomp
15. My Baby Likes to Rock and Roll
16. Strange Pursuit
17. You're My Living Doll
18. Lon Chaney Will Get You If You Don't Watch Out
19. Deed I Do
20. Natural, Natural Baby
21. That's The Way It's Got To Be
22. You Came A Long Way From St. Louis
23. My Love Is Like A Red, Red Rose
24. Goodbye Little Yellow Bird
25. Give Me Love
26. Beautiful Dreamer

A) The Giant Gila Monster
B) I Walked With A Zombie
C) Blood of Dracula
D) Frankenstein's Daughter
E) Hillbillies In A Haunted House
F) How To Make A Monster
G) The Crawling Hand
H) I Was A Teenage Werewolf
I) The Hideous Sun Demon
J) Beginning of the End
K) Horror of Party Beach
L) Hold That Ghost
M) Attack of the Puppet People
N) Eegah
O) The Ghost in the Invisible Bikini
P) Mad Monster Party
Q) The Incredibly Strange Creatures Who Stopped Living and Became Mixed Up Zombies
R) Bela Lugosi Meets A Brooklyn Gorilla
S) Hollywood Revue of 1929
T) The Uninvited
U) Journey to the Center of the Earth
V) Mighty Joe Young
W) Abbottt and Costello Meet the Mummy
X) The Picture of Dorian Gray
Y) Dr. Terror's House of Horrors
Z) Frankenstein Meets the Space Monster

Answers page 142

Monstrous Remakes
Match each monstrous remake with its original film title

1. Creature of Destruction
2. The Bride
3. In the Year 2889
4. Zontar the Thing From Venus
5. The Awakening
6. The Eye Creatures
7. Vengeance
8. Missile to the Moon
9. Stranger from Venus
10. Scared Stiff

A) Invasion of the Saucer Men
B) Donovan's Brain
C) Blood from the Mummy's Tomb
D) Catwomen of the Moon
E) The She Creature
F) Bride of Frankenstein
G) It Conquered the World
H) Day the World Ended
I) The Day the Earth Stood Still
J) The Ghost Breakers

Answers page 143

Monsterous Sports Figures

1. Who played a Manimal in the film Island of Lost Souls and you would also find him in the comic books selling isometric exercises?
2. What pro football star starred alongside Ray Milland in The Thing with Two Heads?
3. Name the British Heavyweight Weightlifting Champion who portrayed the Frankenstein Monster three times
4. Mighty Joe Young gave what one-time heavyweight contender a soaking?
5. Who tries to make a ball player out of Herman on The Munsters TV show?
6. Who played the Diablo Giant and was a prizefighter turned actor?
7. Name the pro wrestler who went from the ring to a mummy film and then a starring role in a feature film
8. Who was Tor Johnson's character in the wrestling arena?
9. Who turned down the opportunity to star as James Bond in Dr. No and held the title of Mr. Universe?
10. What Olympic swimmer turned actor was in projects that used Hal Roach's stock footage from One Million B.C. on three different occasions?

Answers page 134

Mummy's the Word

Match the proper mummy film with its descriptive plot

1. The mummy is in the bayou this time
2. Kharis seeks an ancient medallion
3. Wheeler and Woolsey comedy
4. Kharis seeks vengeance upon archaeologists who disturbed his tomb
5. Imhotep searches for reincarnated princess
6. Amazing Stories TV episode
7. Tom Tyler's only outing as Kharis
8. A 4,000-year-old priest is in search of blood
9. Lugosi as a gangster, smuggles gems inside a mummy
10. Archaeologist Heston's daughter is a reincarnated Egyptian queen
11. The mummy is killed by gunfire and sinks in a swamp
12. An ancient priestess is reincarnated as a New England college student
13. London exhibit meets its demise in an underground sewer
14. Larry, Curly and Moe meet Pharaoh Rutentuten
15. A mummified Seminole witch doctor seeks revenge
16. An expedition to Hamunaptra revives a 3,000-year-old mummy
17. A mummy seeks revenge for the desecration of a pharaoh's tomb

Answers page 143

A) The Mummy's Tomb
B) The Awakening
C) Death Curse of Tartu
D) We Want Our Mummy
E) The Curse of the Mummy's Tomb
F) The Mummy (1932)
G) The Mummy's Curse
H) The Mummy (1959)
I) Mummy Daddy
J) The Mummy (1999)
K) The Mummy's Hand
L) Pharaoh's Curse
M) The Mummy's Shroud
N) The Mummy's Ghost
O) Abbott and Costello Meet the Mummy
P) The Saint's Double Trouble
Q) Mummy's Boys

The 'Way-Out, Wonderful World

Mysterious Plots
Match each mysterious plot with its film title

1. A paralyzing nerve gas and bank robberies
2. A phosphorescent ghost haunts the moors
3. A psychotic killer murders handicapped women
4. The stickpin cemetery murder case
5. A family curse haunts the English moors
6. A mysterious forest, an alien probe and a young teen trapped in another dimension
7. Within the mysterious haunted woods a man is tormented by his past
8. A German castle is the location for mysterious murders
9. A female blackmailer gathers her victims at a seaside house and is murdered
10. Murder in a hatbox
11. A composer commits murder during mental lapses
12. A mad scientist likes to serve a lot of homemade punch
13. A hidden treasure is found by playing notes of "The Marching Men"
14. Moon killer murders leave strangled and mutilated bodies

A) The Red House
B) The Secret of the Blue Room
C) The Hound of the Baskervilles
D) Frankenstein's Daughter
E) The Spiral Staircase
F) Phantom of Crestwood
G) I Bury the Living
H) Dick Tracy Meets Gruesome
I) The Watcher in the Woods
J) Hangover Square
K) The Scarlet Claw
L) Night Must Fall
M) The Ghost Breakers
N) Doctor X

Answers page 143

of Horror, Fantasy and Sci-Fi Movie Trivia   89

No Bones About It
Match each bony creature with its film role

1. Vincent Price uses a skeleton to do in his wife
2. Two teenagers lost in a cave discover the skeleton remains of a missing father
3. Aliens with ray guns leave only the bare bones
4. Peter Cushing is possessed by the Marquis De Sade
5. Lou comes head and shoulders with a skeleton
6. Connie Stevens is frightened by a skeleton gliding down a staircase
7. Ghostly wife scares husband's new bride
8. A parrot hides itself in a skull, frightening The Three Stooges
9. A skeleton is part of a horror-show exhibit
10. Creatures dissolve all flesh down to the bone marrow
11. Kerwin Matthews wields a sword against a skeletal creature
12. Radioactive waste mutates with skeletal remains in the ocean to breed monsters
13. A cadaver is found in a basement
14. A family curse involves decapitation and shrunken heads
15. A villain dons a cape, cowl and a skeleton mask
16. John Carradine controls an army of skeleton-masked monsters
17. Jack Skellington is tired of scare tactics

A) Two on a Guillotine
B) House of Frankenstein
C) House on Haunted Hill
D) If a Body Meets a Body
E) The Horror of Party Beach
F) Teenagers from Outer Space
G) Astro-Zombies
H) Abbott & Costello Meet the Mummy
I) Earth vs. the Spider
J) The Nightmare Before Christmas
K) The Seventh Voyage of Sinbad
L) The Crimson Ghost
M) The Skull
N) Island of Terror
O) The Four Skulls of Jonathan Drake
P) Psycho
Q) The Screaming Skull

Answers page 143

Occupational Pursuits

Before they were stars, actors and actresses were working their way toward stardom. Can you match the following stars with their early occupations?

1. A Manhattan model
2. An accomplished musician
3. A West Point cadet
4. Pursued an engineering degree
5. Trained as a dancer
6. Attended the U.S. Naval Academy at Annapolis, Md.
7. A singing cowboy
8. Studied singing at Warsaw Conservatory in Moscow
9. A U.S. Air Corps sergeant in WWII
10. A truck driver
11. A surveyor's assistant
12. Claimed he had a PHD in child psychology
13. Worked as a stuntman
14. A disc jockey in Dallas
15. Was training to be a military soldier

A) Otto Kruger
B) Robert Paige
C) Elsa Lanchester
D) Boris Karloff
E) Maria Ouspenskaya
F) John Agar
G) Acquanetta
H) Brian Donlevy
I) Glenn Strange
J) Henry Hull
K) Peter Cushing
L) Al Lewis
M) Lou Costello
N) Ted Cassidy
O) Colin Clive

Answers page 143

On A Monster Island With You
Match the following monster islands with their movie titles

1. A yacht full of tourists winds up on an island full of fungus
2. A Nazi scientist experiments on the native girls in order to beautify his wife
3. A rocket crash lands atop a plateau on an island full of dinosaurs
4. A group of people are quarantined on an island with a mysterious plague thought to be the cause of a demon Vrykolakas
5. A mad doctor creates an island full of half men/half beasts
6. An observation balloon is taken by Yankee POWs and lands on an island of giant creatures
7. Boris Karloff becomes involved with native superstitions and a man-eating plant
8. A mad doctor conducts experiments on an island and creates a leopard man
9. A big-game hunter becomes the target after being shipwrecked on an island with a madman who hunts humans
10. Scientists create killer rodents the size of dogs
11. A mad doctor experimenting with chlorophyll accidentally turns his lab assistant into a bloodthirsty creature
12. A plane full of beautiful models and a talent agent crash land on an island where the talent scout is bitten by a giant spider and becomes a monster
13. Dick Foran and Peggy Moran look for treasure on a deserted island in the Florida Keys with a mysterious killer

A) The Lost Continent
B) Mysterious Island
C) The Most Dangerous Game
D) She Demons
E) Isle of the Dead
F) Voodoo Island
G) The Horrors of Spider Island
H) The Killer Shrews
I) Attack of the Mushroom People
J) Island of Lost Souls
K) Mad Doctor of Blood Island
L) Terror is a Man
M) Horror Island

Answers page 143

The Outer Limits
Match each episode title with its profile

1. A spaceship amusement ride becomes the real thing
2. Sand-dwelling creatures attack a space expedition on Mars
3. Alien criminals in a space prison vessel land on Earth
4. POWs are tested for survival tactics with an alien race
5. Alien rocks take possession of humans in order to dominate the Earth
6. Alien parasites infect government officials in an attempt to control the Earth
7. A Welsh miner takes part in an evolution experiment
8. Handicapped children become the focal interest to an alien intelligence
9. A crewmember holds a space station hostage after an alien rainstorm
10. A neighborhood block is transported to another planet for observation
11. A honeymoon gift is inhabited by an alien menace
12. In order to conquer the Earth, an alien is disguised as a boy's tutor
13. Two humans are engaged in a battle of the fittest against two alien lifeforms
14. An attorney tries to help his client (a robot) on a charge of murder
15. An astronaut returns from the planet Venus with a physical imbalance
16. An experiment for world peace causes a man to become an alien life form
17. Murder becomes an experiment for two humanoid Martians
18. A man from Earth's devastated future travels back in time to prevent its destruction
19. A dustball of unknown origin is energized by a vacuum cleaner
20. A South American prehistoric creature is caught and placed on exhibition
21. A robot holds the very thread of Earth's population in his hand
22. Aliens attempt to communicate with an Earth couple by taking the form of tumbleweeds and rocks in the desert
23. Alien swaps intellect for human emotions

Answers page 143

A) The Sixth Finger
B) The Zanti Misfits
C) Second Chance
D) The Invisibles
E) The Mutant
F) The Invisible Enemy
G) A Feasibility Study
H) Nightmare
I) Corpus Earthling
J) The Inheritors
K) Don't Open Till Doomsday
L) Fun and Games
M) I Robot
N) Controlled Experiment
O) The Special One
P) Architects of Fear
Q) Cold Hands Warm Heart
R) The Man Who Was Never Born
S) Tourist Attraction
T) It Crawled Out of the Woodwork
U) Cry of Silence
V) The Demon with a Glass Hand
W) The Keeper of the Purple Twilight

Paul Blaisdell

An imaginative artist, who created many memorable B movie monsters, played the creatures and created special effects for AIP films and others. Match the following film titles with each creative profile Paul gave us.

1. Bloodthirsty alien from Mars
2. Aliens with alcohol
3. A marionette of Dr. Jekyll
4. Paul is seen briefly in a mask in the American version
5. A Halloween party creature
6. Uncredited for his flying bat-creature
7. Monster masks Paul made are displayed
8. Revamped costume makes reappearance
9. Bloodthirsty alien Martian is used again
10. Beulah was its name
11. Just sketched this for Allied Artists
12. Nicknamed creature "Little Hercules"
13. Marty was this mutant's name
14. Interplanetary teleportation controller
15. Uncle Elmo was a mummified corpse
16. Paul creates an oversized syringe
17. Famous creation named "Cuddles"
18. Paul cameoed as a corpse
19. Paul customized a ray gun

A) It Conquered the World
B) The She Creature
C) Invasion of the Saucer Men
D) It The Terror from Beyond Space
E) Voodoo Woman
F) The Ghost of Dragstrip Hollow
G) How to Make a Monster
H) Day The World Ended
I) Not of This Earth
J) Attack of the Puppet People
K) Cat Girl
L) Invisible Invaders
M) From Hell It Came
N) The Beast with a Million Eyes
O) Earth vs. the Spider
P) The Amazing Colossal Man
Q) It Conquered the World
R) Teenagers from Outer Space
S) The Undead

Answers page 143

94 The 'Way-Out, Wonderful World

PRC and Monogram Madness
Match each storyline with its low-budget flick

1. Lugosi commits a murder each time he sees his dead wife
2. A plastic surgeon seeks revenge upon double-crossing Japanese spies
3. Lugosi uses a soup kitchen as a front for murder
4. A doctor seeks a cure for paralysis with the help of a gorilla suit
5. Lugosi and Carradine unleash a frozen Neanderthal man
6. A botanist seeks a cure for his aging wife by stealing brides and using their blood
7. Lugosi seeks a cure for his simian condition
8. Lugosi develops a killer cologne
9. George Zucco turns a farmhand into a werewolf
10. An insurance broker becomes the primary benefactor in murder
11. George Zucco as an innkeeper at a mysterious inn
12. A mad puppeteer/artist strangles women
13. Originally a Universal picture sold to PRC
14. A young girl is framed for murder and convinced she is possessed by her dead father's spirit, who happens to be a mad scientist
15. A ghostly ferryman seeks revenge

A) Invisible Ghost
B) The Brute Man
C) The Ape
D) The Corpse Vanishes
E) Strangler of the Swamp
F) Black Dragons
G) Return of the Ape Man
H) Bowery at Midnight
I) Devil Bat's Daughter
J) The Black Raven
K) The Human Monster
L) The Mad Monster
M) The Ape Man
N) Bluebeard
O) The Devil Bat

Answers page 143

Ray Harryhausen

Stop-motion special effects artist Ray Harryhausen's tremendous accomplishments are known world wide with his giant mythological creatures, monsters from the dawn of time and fantasy worlds. Some Answers are used more than once.

1. The Ymir
2. The Minaton
3. The Selenites
4. The Rhedosaurus
5. A six-tentacle octopus
6. Trog
7. The Griffin
8. Giant crab
9. Medusa
10. Cyclopean Centaur
11. Talos
12. Two-headed Roc
13. Winged Harpies
14. Calibos
15. Giant crocodile
16. The Kraken
17. Triceratops
18. One-horned Cyclops
19. Styracosaurus
20. Seven sworded skeletons

A) Mysterious Island
B) Sinbad and the Eye of the Tiger
C) The Golden Voyage of Sinbad
D) Clash of the Titans
E) Jason and the Argonauts
F) 20 Million Miles to Earth
G) The Seventh Voyage of Sinbad
H) It Came From Beneath the Sea
I) One Million Years B.C.
J) The 3 Worlds of Gulliver
K) First Men in the Moon
L) The Valley of Gwangi
M) The Beast from 20,000 Fathoms

Answers page 143

Robots/Mechanical Marvels

1. Name the 1957 sci-fi film, involving a gigantic energy-eating machine
2. Toho's first alien invasion film involving death rays and gigantic robots
3. What film concerns a malfunctioning computer sabotaging a spaceship's journey to Jupiter?
4. What is the name of the computer in question #3
5. What's the name of the Robot Monster who lands on Earth to wipe out mankind?
6. Name the robot that lived on the planet Altair 4
7. Name Klaatu's seven-foot robot from The Day the Earth Stood Still
8. Name the 1999 animated feature about a nine-year-old boy who saves the life of a giant robot
9. A robot named Chani appeared in this 1954 sci-fi film where Martian women snatch Earthmen for breeding purposes
10. In the film Star Wars what two robots provided the comedy relief
11. Name the robot whose voice was provided by Mel Blanc for Buck Rogers in the 25th Century
12. Name the film in which a father transplants his son's brain after an accident into a robot
13. Name the 1954 film about a mechanical robot which starred Charles Drake
14. What film involves a super computer controlling a missile system?
15. A clumsy robot named Gorgog is involved in what Bowery Boys feature?
16. Vincent Price tries to dominate the world with lady robots. Name the film.
17. Mechanical one-eyed robots chase Jerry Lewis in what Paramount picture?
18. Killer robots from Venus seek out a handful of survivors in a devastated city. Can you name its title?
19. Name the aliens that encase their gelatinous brain-power into cone-shaped robots and oppose Dr. Who
20. An android gunslinger malfunctions and goes on a killing spree at an amusement park. Name the film.
21. Robert Duvall starred in George Lucas' first film involving a future society of robot police. Name the film.

Answers page 134

Sci-Fi/Comedy Horrors

1. What comedy team starred in the horror comedy The Maltese Bippy?
2. In what film would you find a character named Luther Heggs?
3. Name the comedy team that starred in A Haunting We Will Go
4. In what film do Blondie, Dagwood and Baby Dumpling find themselves in a mysterious old mansion?
5. Who played Dr. Einstein in the Frank Capra film Arsenic and Old Lace?
6. Name the musical comedy with Karloff, Lugosi and Lorre.
7. In what film would you find Jerry Lewis as an alien observing the Earth?
8. Don Knotts and Tim Conway are two bungling detectives in a mysterious old manor. Can you name the film?

9. Name the film where Bob Hope is injected with a truth serum and does a Jekyll and Hyde routine.
10. Hope and Crosby have a cameo as skeletons in another comedy teams film. Name the film.
11. What brothers' team did a skit on Mr. Hyde meeting the Frankenstein Monster in the 1936 musical Sing Baby Sing?
12. Scenes from The Walking Dead (1936) are shown in this 1964 comedy with Robert Walker, Jr. What is the movie?
13. Name Lou Costello's only solo film effort.
14. What comedy team starred in the 1941 film Hellzapoppin?
15. Red Skelton plays "The Fox," a radio sleuth involved with a cult of moon worshippers. Name the film.
16. In what film would you find two comedians named Sammy Petrillo and Duke Mitchell meeting Bela Lugosi in a jungle?
17. Dean Jones helps a ghostly pirate do a good deed in this Disney feature.
18. Bob Hope and Willie Best help a beautiful heiress with ghosts in an old Cuban castle. Name this movie.
19. Name the film where an absent-minded professor's chimpanzee mixes up a youth formula causing child regression.
20. In what film would you find The Hudson Brothers being haunted by a lighthouse keeper's corpse?
21. What United Artist film found Elvis Presley and friends being spooked in a ghost town?
22. Tom Hanks stars in this Joe Dante film about a strange family moving into the neighborhood. Name the film.
23. Husband and wife Richard Benjamin and Paula Prentiss move into a haunted house with assorted creatures. Give the film title.
24. What MGM child star played in Francis in the Haunted House?
25. Joan Blondell is a ghost seeking Roland Young's help in finding her murderer. What is the film?
26. Two undertakers try to drum up some business by doing in their landlord. Name this film.
27. The Three Stooges encounter Og and Zog, two Martians invading the Earth. Name the movie.
28. In what film did Moe Howard make his first solo appearance?
29. What brothers team paid tribute to Karloff, Lorre and Laughton in the musical comedy One in a Million?
30. What famous comedian has a small part as a cemetery keeper in the film The Comedy of Terrors?
31. Name the Laurel & Hardy fantasy film that featured the land of the Bogeymen.

Answers page 134 & 135

Simians

1. Name the sequel to the 1976 remake of King Kong
2. Name the chief special effects technician who worked on the original King Kong
3. Name the 1968 film Franklin Schaffner directed, based on a novel by Pierre Boulle
4. Name the Korean film involving a 30-foot ape, who battles a giant white shark
5. Name the title of several screen versions based on a story by W.W. Jacobs
6. In what two films did Acquanetta star in as Paula the ape woman?
7. What was the name of the 3-D film about a carnival gorilla?
8. Bob Burns played Tracy the gorilla in what 1975 comedy series?
9. A botanist turns a chimpanzee into a giant ape in what Herman Cohen film?
10. Name the film where a giant ape rescues children from a burning orphanage
11. Roddy McDowell starred in all but one of the five Planet of the Apes films. Can you name the one he was not in?
12. In what film did two famous monsters battle on the top of Mount Fuji?
13. Name the 1933 film about a giant white ape named Kiko
14. Name the 1954 Warner Bros. film starring Steve Forrest that was a remake of a 1932 Lugosi classic
15. In what film does a circus owner discover a giant ape?
16. Name the 1953 Jungle Jim film with Ray "Crash" Corrigan as a simian beast
17. In what film would you find J. Carrol Naish as an ape turned human?
18. Nazis disguise themselves as gorillas in this Jungle Jim film

Answers page 135

Spacecraft

1. Name the spacecraft that was the home of the Robinson family for three years
2. In the film 2001: A Space Odyssey, what was the spaceship's name?
3. Lloyd Bridges and crew blast off for the Moon only to land on Mars. The ship's name is in the title.
4. Name the spacecraft Sigourney Weaver and crew are attacked on in Alien
5. Name the spacecraft in the Irwin Allen TV show Land of the Giants
6. In what sci-fi television series would you find Skydiver One?
7. What's the name of the shuttlecraft in the original Star Trek episode where Spock and crew were marooned on Taurus II?
8. Name the 1962 TV outer space adventure series with Steve Zodiac and crew. (Hint: the ship's name is in the title.)
9. Name the film about a space probe with an alien fungus. (Hint: Moe Howard has a part in the film.)
10. Grand Moff Tarkin (Peter Cushing) is at the helm of this space battleship
11. A scout ship is on a mission to destroy unstable suns that are about to super nova
12. What is the name of Han Solo's spacecraft?
13. What's Luke Skywalker's favorite spacecraft?

Answers page 135

Scream Queens
Match each scream queen with her profile

1. Universal fans favorite scream queen
2. Starred in several macabre films with Lionel Atwill
3. She played Minnie in Bride of Frankenstein
4. Starred in Fred Olen Ray's Haunting Fear
5. Vincent Price seeks to add her to his wax museum
6. Peter Lorre falls madly in love with her
7. She played Anna in Frankenstein Must Be Destroyed
8. She played opposite Clint Eastwood and Richard Burton in Where Eagles Dare
9. She was threatened by The Werewolf of London
10. She played opposite Dwight Frye and Bela Lugosi
11. She's been up against a grapefruit and the Frankenstein Monster
12. She was Count Mora's daughter Luna
13. She was Gladys DuCane in The Old Dark House
14. Bela Lugosi as Dr. Vollin was obsessed with her
15. She won a contest to play the panther woman
16. She is best remembered as Dracula's Daughter
17. She played Ivy opposite Fredric March
18. She endured hungry lions and Karl Freund
19. She was the bride of Karloff on film but was really married to Charles Laughton
20. She was in two James Whale horror films and won an Oscar in Titanic
21. She was in the 1934 film The Black Cat

A) Mae Clarke
B) Irene Ware
C) Fay Wray
D) Gloria Stuart
E) Miriam Hopkins
F) Evelyn Ankers
G) Elsa Lanchester
H) Brinke Stevens
I) Una O'Conner
J) Frances Drake
K) Helen Chandler
L) Ingrid Pitt
M) Valerie Hobson
N) Veronica Carlson
O) Phyllis Kirk
P) Kathleen Burke
Q) Zita Johann
R) Carroll Borland
S) Gloria Holden
T) Lillian Bond
U) Jacqueline Wells

Answers page 143

Spooky Radio

1. Who annihilated the world on October 30, 1938?
2. A squeaking door and a host by the name of Raymond beckoned you to what horror radio program?
3. Lugosi appeared on what mystery program which featured the story "The Doctor Prescribed Death"?
4. What 1950s radio program had Commander Buzz Cory and Cadet Happy, who traveled the solar system?
5. On what show would a voice proclaim, "It's later than you think"?
6. What comedian did a spoof on horror radio shows with "The Chicken Heart" on a 1960s record album?
7. An old hermit would beckon you into his dark abode, where weird stories of ghosts and murders were told — name this program
8. The bell-keeper tolled his bell in his cave by the restless sea, announcing bizarre stories and weird tales. The bell would toll for what radio program?
9. This star of many 1950s sci-fi films appeared on radio with Lucille Ball in My Favorite Husband — name him
10. Who sang "We're Horrible, Horrible Men" on Bakers Broadcast, October 31, 1938?

Answers page 135

Star Treatment

1. What two horror actors share the same birthday on May 27?
2. What horror film actor passed away on August 16, 1956?
3. How many films did Boris Karloff and Bela Lugosi appear in together?
4. True or false: Bela Lugosi was buried in one of his Dracula capes
5. Name the only horror film in which Humphrey Bogart starred
6. Barbara Stanwyck has nightmares that her late husband is trying to kill her
7. Evelyn Ankers was married to what 1950s sci-fi film star?
8. Name the only horror/fantasy film in which Carole Lombard appeared
9. Name the four horror actors who were honored on a U.S. postage stamp in 1997
10. In what film would you find Ernest Thesiger as an undertaker?
11. Who played Mr. Gateman on the TV series The Munsters?
12. Name the sci-fi films in which Peter Graves starred
13. What Hollywood director did Ian McKellen portray in Gods and Monsters?
14. George "The Animal" Steele portrayed what larger than life actor?
15. What Sam Cooke song is Frankenstein mentioned in?
16. In Rocketeer one of the villains resembles what Universal horror actor?
17. Who played Mr. Waverly on The Man from U.N.C.L.E. and was in Topper and Tarantula?
18. What Lon Chaney, Sr. role did Chaney, Jr. want, but did not get, in the remake?
19. In what MGM sci-fi classic did Disney animators animate an alien beast?
20. In It's Only Money with Jerry Lewis, a murderer (Jack Weston) is the president of what horror actor's fan club?
21. Matinee pays homage to what horror producer/director?
22. What actress portrayed the Spider Woman in Sherlock Holmes and the Spider Woman and The Spider Woman Strikes Back?
23. In the film Abbott and Costello Meet the Invisible Man, whose picture is seen on the wall in Dr. Gray's office?
24. Who played a werewolf butler on an episode of The Lucy Show with Vivian Vance and Lucille Ball as witches?
25. Who played Dr. Phibes' dead wife in the two Phibes films?
26. Who played Sandor in Dracula's Daughter and directed Destination Moon?
27. Who created the electrical equipment used in the 1931 Frankenstein?
28. Name the child star who appeared in several horror/sci-fi films of the 1950s and 1960s including The Fly, Them and 13 Ghosts
29. What horror actor's daughter shares the same birthday as her famous father?
30. What actor was horror host Al Gory in a 1993 drama co-starring Gary Sinise?
31. What actor from the The Vampire appeared on TV's Dark Shadows?
32. While a waitress, Sally Kellerman co-wrote what film script with Roger Corman?
33. In the 1931 film Dracula, who spoke the very first lines in the film?
34. What actor from Jaws made his film debut in The Curse of the Living Corpse?
35. In The Return of Count Yorga, what 1990s TV star plays a police detective?
36. What horror actor in 1935 lived in a house above the Hollywoodland sign?

37. Who played two of the aviators that shot down King Kong from the Empire State Building?
38. Name the actress who starred in the film Ghost Ship with her first husband Dermot Walsh. (Hint: She starred in several films with Vincent Price)
39. Name the actress who was cast in the title role in the Hammer production of Vampirella, which unfortunately was never produced.
40. What silent screen actor appeared in The Phantom Planet as Sesom, the ruler of a mobile asteroid?
41. In the film Bluebeard, what is significant about one of John Carradine's victims played by Sonia Sorel?
42. What horror actor recorded a hymn called "He Is There"
43. What acclaimed director declined to do the narration for the film War of the Worlds?
44. What independent film director from the 1920s and 1930s was suspected of being involved in the death of film actress Thelma Todd? (Hint: he directed The Bat and The Bat Whispers.)
45. Who starred in The Thirteenth Guest and became a famous star in musicals?
46. Name the director who gave Peter Cushing his first film role
47. Who was the first Hollywood star to publicly announce having a drug problem?
48. Name the actor who played a werewolf and was also a member of the original singing group The Lettermen.
49. What studio in 1932 released the first sound and color monster movie?
50. Name the only color film in which Bela Lugosi starred.

Answers pages 135 & 136

Teenage Horrors

Match each teenager with the sci-fi /horror film in which they appeared
(may be more than one answer)

1. The Horror of It All
2. Panic in Year Zero
3. My Blood Runs Cold
4. The Ghost in the Invisible Bikini
5. Two on a Guillotine
6. Space Children
7. Tickle Me
8. Dr. Goldfoot and the Girl Bombs
9. How to Make a Monster
10. I Was a Teenage Werewolf
11. War Gods of the Deep
12. Village of the Giants
13. The Blob
14. Eegah
15. Queen of Blood
16. Teenage Caveman
17. Dr. Goldfoot and the Bikini Machine
18. War of the Gargantuans

A) Johnny Crawford
B) Fabian
C) Michael Landon
D) Tab Hunter
E) Steve McQueen
F) Robert Vaughn
G) Tommy Kirk
H) Arch Hall, Jr.
I) Dean Jones
J) Russ Tamblyn
K) Elvis Presley
L) Pat Boone
M) John Ashley
N) Troy Donahue
O) John Saxon
P) Frankie Avalon
Q) Dwayne Hickman
R) Beau Bridges

Answers page 143

Titans of Horror

It has been noted that with one great horror actor a film can be a classic, but with the teaming of two, or three or even four legends, the combination is beyond belief. Match the following team of horror actors with the film title they appeared in together.

1. Karloff, Price, Rathbone and Lorre
2. Lorre, Lugosi and Karloff
3. Lorre, Karloff and Price
4. Carradine, Price, Lee and Cushing
5. Rathbone, Chaney, Jr., Lugosi, Carradine and Johnson
6. Karloff, Atwill, Chaney, Jr., Carradine, Strange and Naish
7. Lugosi, Chaney, Jr., Strange, and Price
8. Carradine, Rathbone and Chaney, Jr.
9. Karloff, Lugosi, Rathbone and Atwill
10. Chaney, Jr., Lugosi, Atwill and Frye
11. Carradine, Chaney, Jr., Strange, and Atwill
12. Chaney, Jr., Lugosi, Atwill and Hardwicke
13. Karloff, Chaney, Jr. and Lorre
14. Rathbone, Price and Lorre
15. Karloff and Rathbone
16. Karloff and Lorre

A) The Ghost in the Invisible Bikini
B) The Black Sleep
C) The Boogie Man Will Get You
D) Lizard's Legs and Owlet's Wing
E) You'll Find Out
F) The Raven
G) Frankenstein Meets the Wolfman
H) The Comedy of Terrors
I) House of Dracula
J) The Ghost of Frankenstein
K) Abbott and Costello Meet Frankenstein
L) House of the Long Shadows
M) Son of Frankenstein
N) House of Frankenstein
O) Hillbillies in a Haunted House
P) Tales of Terror

Answers page 144

of Horror, Fantasy and Sci-Fi Movie Trivia

To Bee or Not To Bee

1. Name the film where wasp enzymes become an eternal youth formula
2. John Saxon and John Carradine are out to stop South American killer bees.
3. In what 1973 sci-fi flick do beautiful women receive a dose of radiation that transforms them into deadly queen bees?
4. Name The Outer Limits episode involving a beautiful woman that is actually a queen bee
5. What is the Monster from Green Hell?
6. Name the Irwin Allen film about killer bees that starred Henry Fonda and Richard Widmark
7. Name the film where a giant honeybee encloses a couple in a honeycomb
8. What Bert I. Gordon film along with giant rats and chickens has also giant wasps?
9. Name the Disney film where a shrunken child takes a ride on a giant bumblebee
10. Which Sinbad film featured a giant bee?
11. This 1966 film stars Suzanna Leigh and is about a beekeeper and his trained bees.
12. TV movie involving a family of winemakers and bees starring Gloria Swanson
13. Insects attack during the Mardi Gras in New Orleans in what 1976 TV movie?

Answers page 136

TV Horror Hosts

With the release of the Shock! package to television in 1957, a new generation of kids were exposed to the original Universal horror classics. Local horror hosts became essential in promoting these films as they cast their spell on a whole new generation of kids. Match the following horror host with his/her correct identity.

1. 1950s horror host known as "The Cool Ghoul"
2. Washington D.C. Creature Features host
3. Had a small cameo in Night of the Living Dead
4. L.A. horror hostess Cassandra Peterson
5. Had a hit record and starred in his own movie
6. Known as "Sir Cecil Creape"
7. Originated in Detroit on WJBK, Channel 2 in 1967. Later picked up by a Cleveland station and WTOP Channel 9 in Washington DC
8. Recorded "The Transylvania Twist"
9. Undertaker from St. Petersburg, Florida
10. Hosted Monsterpiece Theatre in Fairfax, Virginia
11. Had a fan club called "The Slimy Wall Times"
12. Kansas City's own "ghostess with the mostess"
13. Had a weekly segment called "Parma Place"
14. This horror host would be heard to say: "Shock-tails for two" on WBAL TV in Baltimore, Maryland
15. Wyatt Earp in The Three Stooges film The Outlaws is Coming
16. Host from Philadelphia, who resembled W.C. Fields
17. She played a hag in Bert I. Gordon's The Magic Sword
18. Conjured up a mummy played by Bob Burns in 1962

A) Dr. Shock
B) Bowman Body
C) Gorgon
D) Dr. Lucifer
E) Zacherley
F) Vampira
G) Ghoulardi
H) Dr. Paul Bearer
I) Seymour
J) Crematia Mortem
K) The Phantom of the Opry
L) Sir Graves Ghastly
M) Morgus the Magnificent
N) Baron Daemon
O) Chilly Billy
P) Elvira
Q) Count Gore DeVol
R) Jeepers Creepers

Answers page 144

TV Horrors - Dark Shadows

1. What TV network did the original Dark Shadows appear on?
2. Which of the following dates is the correct TV debut for the original series:
    A) June 25, 1965   B) June 27, 1966   C) April 28, 1967
3. Who produced the series?
4. How did the producer come up with the idea for Dark Shadows?
5. Name the manor estate where the Collins family lived.
6. Name the governess who tutors the young Collins child.
7. In April 1967 what predominant character joined the cast?
8. In the opening credits what scene is depicted?
9. Name the witch who places a curse of vampirism on a Collins member
10. Name the two actresses who played Dr. Hoffman in the original and the revised series
11. What Collins family member was both a ghost and a werewolf?
12. Name the place where Josette DuPree lost her life.
13. Name the composer for the Dark Shadows eerie theme.
14. What Hollywood legend played Elizabeth Collins Stoddard in the original series?
15. How many Dark Shadows motion pictures were produced?
16. What is the name of the local hot spot for dancing and dining in Collinsport?
17. Quentin's Theme was originally in another Dan Curtis production. Can you name the TV movie?
18. Who recited the closing voice-over on the final episode:
    A) Jonathan Frid   B) David Selby   C) Thayer David
19. A group called The Vampire State Building had a novelty song inspired by the series. What was its title?

Answers page 136

Television Horrors
Match each episode title with its TV show

1. Beach Head
2. The Keeper
3. The Incredible Dr. Markesan
4. The Galaxy Being
5. The After Hours
6. The Winged Avenger
7. The Ghost of A. Chantz
8. Moment of Hate
9. Spectre of the Gun
10. I Was a Teenage Monster
11. Trick or Treat
12. Space Vampire
13. Girl on the Road
14. The Haunted House
15. Zombie Terror
16. I Was a Middle-Aged Werewolf
17. The Ghost Wolf
18. The Bat Cave Affair
19. Horror in the Heights
20. The Haunted House
21. V is for Vampire
22. Up at Bat
23. Fright Night
24. The Night of the Wolf
25. The Greatest Monster of Them All
26. Werewolf

A) The Dick Van Dyke Show
B) One Step Beyond
C) The Outer Limits
D) The Monkees
E) Abbott and Costello Show
F) The Man From Uncle
G) Star Trek
H) The Andy Griffith Show
I) Ramar of the Jungle
J) The Invaders
K) Gilligan's Island
L) Boris Karloff's Thriller
M) Buck Rogers in the 25th Century
N) Lost in Space
O) The Beverly Hillbillies
P) The Avengers
Q) The Twilight Zone
R) Highway to Heaven
S) Kolchak the Night Stalker
T) The Veil
U) F-Troop
V) The Adventures of Superman
W) Voyage to the Bottom of the Sea
X) Alfred Hitchcock Presents
Y) Rod Serling's Night Gallery
Z) Wild Wild West

Answers page 144

The 'Way-Out, Wonderful World

TV Horrors - Out of This World Pilots
Match the descriptive pilot with its title

1. Boris Karloff hosted this Hal Roach-proposed pilot
2. Curt Siodmak wrote and directed this pilot
3. Jack Arnold directed this pilot about a couple renting a house haunted by the ghost of George Armstrong Custer
4. Darren McGavin is against an evil witch
5. Vincent Price hosted an edited version of the film Tormented
6. John Saxon plays a 20th-century scientist captured by a society of women
7. A Greenwich Village apartment is the residence of a vampiric lawyer, a beautiful witch and other gruesome residents
8. Alan Alda adopts an invisible baby left on his doorstep
9. A black ghost haunts a colonial mansion occupied by a white family
10. This pilot was a spin-off from a Twilight Zone episode
11. Ron Howard wishes for a fairy godmother—only to get Bert Lahr as his fairy godfather
12. The ghost of a private investigator helps a detective agency owned by his son and daughter
13. Keenan Wynn plays a ghost in a New England mansion
14. Shelley Long and Barry Van Dyke are haunted by the ghost of Shelley's first husband
15. Dick Shawn and Paula Prentiss are vampires
16. Robert Vaughn creates a creature

A) Where's Everett?
B) Ghost of a Chance
C) Planet Earth
D) The Veil
E) Witchcraft
F) Mr. Bevis
G) Tales of Frankenstein
H) 13 Thirteenth Avenue
I) Who Goes There?
J) Freeman
K) Gumshoes
L) Jeremiah of Jacobs Neck
M) Barnaby
N) Famous Ghost Stories
O) Doctor Franken
P) Mr. and Mrs. Dracula

Answers page 144

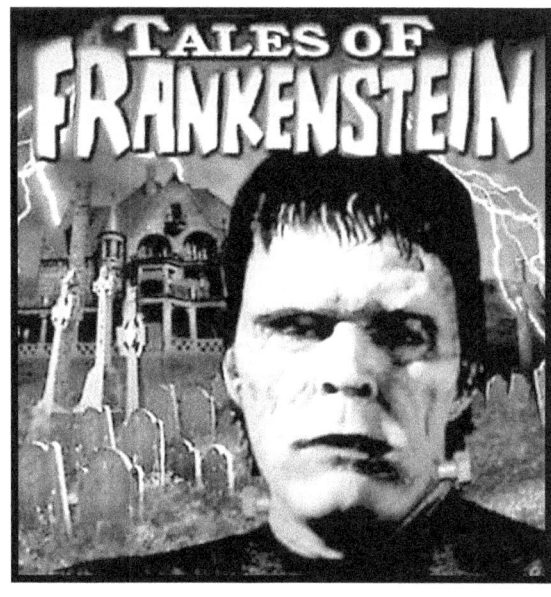

TV Terrors

1. What was the name of Morticia's African Strangler plant on The Addams Family?
2. Name Lurch's famous spoken line on The Addams Family
3. What was the name of Wednesday Addams' headless doll?
4. What television horror series did Stephen King say was the best ever aired?
5. What horror actor played the villain Egghead on the television series Batman?
6. On The Andy Griffith Show episode "Three Wishes For Opie," what is the name of the Count who grants Opie's three requests?
7. Who supposedly haunts "The Haunted House" episode on The Andy Griffith Show?
8. What ghost supposedly haunts a cabin on an episode of The Dick Van Dyke Show

9. What does Ritchie Cunningham see in an old house that is the site of Ralph Malph's annual Halloween party?
10. What does William Shatner see in The Twilight Zone episode "Nightmare At 20,000 Feet"?
11. What is the name of the painting that attacks William Shatner in an episode of Boris Karloff's Thriller? (Hint: It's also the episodes title.)
12. What television series had an episode with Lara Parker (Angelique from Dark Shadows) mixed up with live mannequins?
13. What is the name of Eddie Munster's doll?
14. In the episode "Will Success Spoil Herman Munster," what is the name of the song Herman records that becomes a sensation?

15. Who was the narrator for the television series Way Out?
16. What was the name of the television show that featured Bob Cummings and a lovely robot played by Julie Newmar?
17. Who was your guide into the world of the unknown on One Step Beyond?
18. Name the television series filmed in Sweden that featured Lon Chaney, Jr. as its host

The 'Way-Out, Wonderful World

19. Fill in the blank to this unsold TV horror anthology: "Good evening. Tonight I'm going to tell you another strange and unusual story of the unexplainable which lies behind…"
20. The instrumental "Funeral March of A Marionette" was from what TV series?
21. Name the science patrol officer who became Ultraman in 1966
22. Who was responsible for the special effects on Ultraman?
23. Name the rock group who played themselves on The Munsters in the TV episode "Far Out Munsters."

Answers page 136

Underwater Monstrosities
Match each monster movie title with its monstrous plot

1. On the coast of Mexico a one-eyed octopus terrorizes a village
2. An atomic half-alligator, half-turtle mutant protects a uranium deposit
3. Bloodthirsty creatures store victims for their food supply in an underwater cavern
4. A space alien terrorizes an underwater lab
5. A submarine searches for a UFO and finds it inhabited by a one-eyed invader
6. Giant mollusks mutated by radiation attack Western hero Tim Holt
7. A lighthouse keeper plays nursemaid to a sea creature
8. Doug McClure finds himself in an undersea kingdom ruled by Martians
9. A mad scientist turns into a walking catfish
10. A giant squid attacks a submarine crew
11. A giant octopus snags the Golden Gate Bridge
12. An oceanographer poses as a seaweed creature to murder bikini-clad girls
13. To steal gold a gangster invents a sea monster, then meets a real one in the ocean
14. Radioactive waste creates sea monsters

A) ZAAT
B) The Monster that Challenged the World
C) Monster of Piedras Blancas
D) Warlords of Atlantis
E) Monster from the Ocean Floor
F) 20,000 Leagues Under the Sea
G) It Came from Beneath the Sea
H) Phantom from 10,000 Leagues
I) Atomic Submarine
J) Destination Inner Space
K) Attack of the Giant Leeches
L) Creature from the Haunted Sea
M) The Horror of Party Beach
N) Monster from the Surf

Answers page 144

Vampires
Match the following actors with their vampire names

1. Webb Fallon
2. Armand Tesla
3. Baron Latos
4. Drake Robey
5. Dr. Ravna
6. Baron Meinster
7. Paul Johnson
8. Count Mora
9. Dr. Elwyn Clayton
10. Janos Skorzeny
11. Dr. Paul Beecher
12. Blacula
13. Count Yorga
14. Dr. Callistrastus
15. Bellac Goudal
16. Count Von Krolock

A) John Carradine
B) Noel Willman
C) Paul Birch
D) Bela Lugosi
E) George Zucco
F) Michael Pate
G) John Beal
H) Bela Lugosi
I) David Peel
J) William Marshall
K) John Abbott
L) Francis Lederer
M) Barry Atwater
N) Robert Quarry
O) Donald Wolfit
P) Ferdy Mayne

Answers page 144

Variety of Horrors

Match each horror guest appearance with its variety show

1. Karloff sings "It Was A Very Good Year"
2. A Dr. Jekyll and Mr. Hyde skit
3. Glenn Strange appears as the Frankenstein Monster
4. Lon Chaney, Jr. as the Frankenstein Monster
5. Fred Gwynne as Herman Munster has a guest appearance
6. Christopher Lee is paid tribute
7. Ted Cassidy and Boris Karloff appeared together on October 30, 1965
8. Karloff and Price sing "The Two of Us"
9. Lon Chaney, Jr. plays the Wolfman in the sketch "The Curse of the Wolfman"
10. A television show called "Shriek Theater" causes havoc on this show
11. Tony Curtis as Dracula meets Frank Gorshin
12. Storybook time with Uncle Boris was highlighted
13. Lugosi demonstrates his vampire bat illusion trick
14. Boris sings "Mama Look A Boo Boo"
15. Steve Allen plays a vampire in a sketch with his wife Jayne Meadows
16. Gabe Dell plays Dracula with assistant Ygor (Don Knotts)
17. Basil Rathbone guest starred on this show in 1958

A) The Danny Kaye Show
B) The Pat Boone Show
C) Shindig
D) The Jonathan Winters Show
E) The Red Skelton Show
F) This Is Your Life
G) The Jack Benny Show
H) The Tex Williams Show
I) The Colgate Comedy Hour
J) The Phil Silvers Show
K) You Asked For It
L) The ABC Comedy Hour
M) The Chevy Show with Dinah Shore
N) The Milton Berle Show
O) The Rosemary Clooney Show
P) The Steve Allen Show
Q) The Betty White Show

Answers page 144

Way Out There

1. What is the name of the inn Jack Griffin arrives at in The Invisible Man?
2. Who played Babe Jensen in The Mummy's Hand and its sequel?
3. In what sci-fi film would you find an actor named David Love?
4. What AIP monster appeared on TV in Quinn's Corner and Campus Club?
5. Jack Palance as Jack the Ripper uses the pseudonym Mr. Slade in this 1954 film
6. What sci-fi classic features Woody Woodpecker giving space flight technology?
7. Who played Juliandra from planet Herculon on TV in Rocky Jones Space Ranger
8. Who owned the chamber of horrors (actor & character) in House of Frankenstein
9. Name of the prison housing Dr. Niemann and Daniel in House of Frankenstein?
10. In what 1930s film was the wall from King Kong used as a burning building?
11. What sci-fi writer visited the set of Warner Bros.' 1936 The Walking Dead?
12. Name the café from the film The Mummy's Curse?
13. Name of the book that Norman Reed (Lon Chaney, Jr.) wrote in Weird Woman
14. Name the cemetery Turhan Bey is the caretaker for in The Mummy's Tomb
15. Name the collector of ectoplasmic spirits in 13 Ghosts
16. What 1960s television series featured highlights of the film Reptilicus?
17. In the pilot for The Munsters, what was the name of Herman's wife and who played her?
18. What is the name of the giant lobster dragon in the 1936 Flash Gordon serial?
19. In what 1965 Allied Artist film would you find a space monster named Mull?
20. Name the planet from which Paul Birch is from in Not of this Earth
21. What horror actor was in a Lost in Space episode entitled "The Galaxy Gift"?
22. Who played Rod Brown of the Rocket Rangers on TV?
23. What does the giant space alien steal from Allison Hayes in Attack of the 50 Foot Woman?
24. In the film The Premature Burial, what is the haunting melody that disturbs Ray Milland?
25. Who co-hosted the CBS Thanksgiving Day Special with Burl Ives on November 24, 1955?
26. What 1932 horror movie poster sold at Sotheby's in Manhattan for $453,500 — one of the most expensive Hollywood movie posters sold to date?
27. In the film The Howling, what is significant about the name on the degree hanging on the wall in the doctor's office?
28. What radio personality did an off-screen narration for the film Lobster Man from Mars in 1988?

Answers page 137

Werewolves

1. In what film would you find the Mariphasa Lupina Lumino?
2. Who stars as the gypsy woman in The Wolfman and Frankenstein Meets the Wolfman?
3. Name the film where Nina Foch plays Celeste La Tour
4. Name the actor who played Andreas Obry, a werewolf who helps a vampire (Lugosi) in Return of the Vampire
5. Name the film where June Lockhart believes she is a werewolf
6. Name the 1960 film that was loosely based on "The Werewolf of Paris" by Guy Endore
7. Name the film where a superintendent for a girls' reform school is actually a werewolf
8. In what 1956 film concerns two scientists using an experimental drug on an accident victim that turns the victim into a werewolf?
9. What film would you find Larry Talbot (Lon Chaney, Jr.) supposedly cured of his werewolf habits?
10. Name of film in which Barry McGuire (singer of "Eve of Destruction") appeared

Answers page 137

What A Steele

The lovely Barbara Steele is well known among monster boomers. Can you match her film titles with the film plots?

1. Victims from the Black Plague begin to rise from their graves
2. A 17th-century witch is revived by a drop of blood
3. A research scientist helps to aid a vampire's curse
4. A doctor's second wife is haunted by the ghost of his first wife, whom he accidentally killed
5. Steele, in a dual role—as a ghost and her cousin
6. A man makes a wager with Edgar Allan Poe to spend the night in a haunted castle. Steele plays a bloodthirsty ghost.
7. Steele is haunted by her husband's ghost, who seeks revenge for her unfaithfulness
8. Steele portrays the daughter of a woman burned at the stake for witchcraft
9. Barbara is possessed by a witch in Transylvania
10. A Canadian apartment complex is plagued by parasitic bugs
11. Barbara drives her husband insane using his father's evil past
12. Steele is a military officer
13. Steele portrays a witch in a film that stars Boris Karloff and Christopher Lee

A) The Ghost
B) The Crimson Cult
C) Piranha
D) Shivers
E) The Horrible Dr. Hitchcock
F) Nightmare Castle
G) Castle of Blood
H) Black Sunday
I) Dark Shadows
J) The She Beast
K) Terror Creatures from the Grave
L) The Long Hair of Death
M) The Pit and the Pendulum

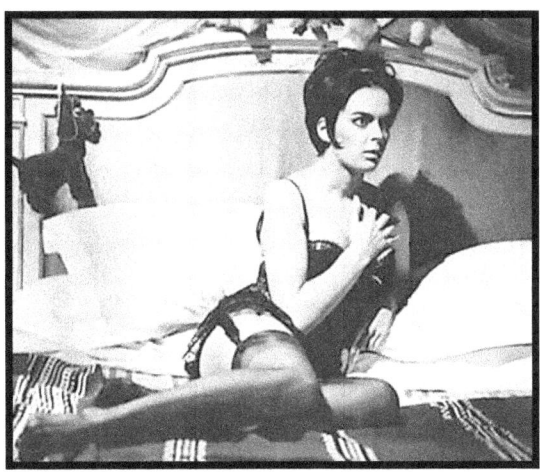

Answers page 144

What's In A Number?
Match each story line with the numbered film title.

1. Ken Clark and Tom Conway land on the Moon and discover that moon creatures want to freeze the Earth
2. Five Earthlings are given capsules from an alien race that could destroy the Earth
3. Lon Chaney, Jr. stars in this film as Tomack
4. An alien spaceship is unearthed in London with corpses of Martian grasshoppers
5. A future world is under governmental dictatorship
6. A phantom ship with deceased passengers
7. James Arness' 1950 film involving pirates and dinosaurs
8. An inventor turns his fiancée into a giant
9. A statue of the goddess of love comes to life
10. 1974 film involving intelligent ants and world domination
11. Francis Ford Coppola's film about an axe murderer on an Irish estate
12. Rosey Grier and Ray Milland bond together
13. A beautiful Asian woman diabolically kills her ex-sorority sisters
14. Bruce Dern as a mad scientist in this 1970 effort
15. Ray Bradbury story about book-burning persecutors

A) Thirteen Women
B) 1984
C) One Touch of Venus
D) Two Lost Worlds
E) One Million B.C.
F) Between Two Worlds
G) The 30-Foot Bride of Candy Rock
H) 12 to the Moon
I) The 27th Day
J) Five Million Years To Earth
K) Fahrenheit 451
L) The Incredible Two-Headed Transplant
M) Phase 4
N) The Thing with Two Heads
O) Dementia 13
Answers page 144

The 'Way-Out, Wonderful World

What's In Common With
Discover what similarities there are in the three hints below

1. Plan Nine From Outer Space, The Magic Sword and actress Lisa Marie
2. Charlie Chan at the Opera, Fu Manchu and Dr. Yogami
3. Carousel, The Unearthly and Don Post masks
4. Konga, Horror of Dracula and Alfred the butler
5. The Mummy's Ghost, House of Horrors and the Caped Crusader
6. Munster Go Home, The Night Strangler and a New York restaurant
7. Nigel Green, Arnold Schwarzenegger and Gordon Scott
8. David Warner, Jack Palance and Laird Cregar
9. Charles Bronson, Marie Antoinette and Joan of Arc
10. The Fly, Felix Leiter and the Seaview
11. Lee Merriweather, Veronica Hamel and Ann Magnuson
12. Kerwin Matthews, Patrick Wayne and John Philip Law
13. Revenge of the Creature, Tarantula and Rawhide
14. Frankenstein and the Monster From Hell, Horror of Frankenstein and Darth Vader
15. Klaus Kinski, Max Schreck and Willem Dafoe
16. Omar Sharif, Herbert Lom and Robert Ryan
17. My Mom's A Werewolf, The Time Travelers and Queen of Blood
18. Ilona Massey, Valerie Hobson and Mae Clarke
19. Ian Richardson, Peter Cushing and Christopher Lee
20. Burt Lancaster, Antonio Banderas and Maxmillian Schell
21. The Old Dark House, Night of the Hunter and Quasimodo
22. Boris Karloff, Christopher Lee and Peter Sellers
23. Peter Cushing, Sir Laurence Olivier and Herbert Lom
24. Daughter of Dr. Jekyll, X the Man with the X-Ray Eyes and The Thing from Another World
25. William Shatner, Joe Dante and Dick Miller
26. The Burbs, The Ghost and Mr. Chicken and Alfred Hitchcock Presents episode "Bang Your Dead"
27. Frankenstein, Jr., an android (on the original Star Trek series) and Thing (The Addams Family)

Answers page 137

Where Monsters Die

Match each movie with the location where its monster met its doom

1. Manhattan Tunnel in New York
2. Empire State Building in N.Y.
3. Hoover Dam in Nevada
4. Big Ben in London
5. Griffith Park Observatory in L.A.
6. Westminster Cathedral in London
7. The Roman Colosseum
8. Around Washington D.C.'s landmarks
9. The Atlantic Ocean
10. Inside the Griffith Park Observatory, Los Angeles
11. Lake Michigan
12. The Brooklyn Bridge in New York

A) Phantom from Space
B) Konga
C) The Creeping Unknown
D) The Giant Claw
E) War of the Colossal Beast
F) Earth vs. the Flying Saucers
G) The Deadly Mantis
H) The Amazing Colossal Man
I) King Kong
J) 20 Million Miles to Earth (Ymir)
K) Godzilla (1998)
L) Beginning of the End (Giant Grasshoppers)

Answers page 144

The Year Is
Match the correct year with the following descriptions

1. Boris Karloff appears on the cover of Life magazine and Dracula Has Risen From the Grave is in theaters
2. 20 Million Miles to Earth is released and James Whale dies
3. Raquel Welch appears in One Million Years B.C. and Star Trek comes to TV
4. Destination Moon wins an Academy Award for special effects and The Day the Earth Stood Still is released
5. Conrad Brooks is born and Dracula is released
6. Elena Verdugo is born and Willis O'Brien's The Lost World is released
7. The Time Machine wins an Academy Award for special effects and Aurora's Frankenstein model is in stores
8. Mighty Joe Young receives an Academy Award for special effects and Rocketship X-M lands in theaters
9. Kolchak The Night Stalker (TV series) is televised and you can Escape To Witch Mountain in theaters
10. War of the Worlds wins an Academy Award for special effects and Godzilla makes his film debut
11. Matinee is released to theaters as well as Carnosaur
12. Frankenstein Meets the Wolfman is released and Lewis Wilson portrays Batman in a 15-chapter serial
13. Alfred Hitchcock Presents comes to TV and It Came From Beneath the Sea is on the big screen
14. Fredric March wins an Academy Award for Dr. Jekyll and Mr. Hyde and Boris Karloff is in The Mummy
15. Bela Lugosi dies this year and Beast of Hollow Mountain is released

A) 1932
B) 1966
C) 1925
D) 1968
E) 1950
F) 1974
G) 1961
H) 1943
I) 1956
J) 1955
K) 1954
L) 1931
M) 1993
N) 1957
O) 1951

Answers page 144

You Know Bruno

Bruno VeSota or De Sota was an actor known for playing heavies in B-films and was also featured in various AIP pictures. Match the following descriptive plots and see if you know Bruno.

1. Bruno directed this film about an invasion of beautiful aliens and their vegetable monsters
2. Bruno stars as Dave Walker, husband to Liz baby
3. Bruno co-starred in this film with Dennis Hopper
4. Bruno plays a night watchman attacked by Susan Cabot
5. Bruno directed this sci-fi film loosely based on Robert A. Heinlein's The Puppet Masters
6. Bruno receives a massage while getting the facts about a mad scientist's evil past
7. Bruno costarred in this Roger Corman sci-fi film about aliens attempting to stop a manned spaceship flight
8. Bruno is a bartender in a New England town
9. Bruno portrays a man named Scroop in this film about witchcraft
10. Bruno directed this film under one of its titles, Dementia

A) War of the Satellites
B) The Haunted Palace
C) Invasion of the Star Creatures
D) Night Tide
E) Creature of the Walking Dead
F) The Wasp Woman
G) Attack of the Giant Leeches
H) The Brain Eaters
I) The Undead
J) Daughter of Horror

Answers page 144

Zombies
Match each film title with its profile

1. Zombified bride of Carradine
2. Sometimes thought of as "Jane Eyre in the West Indies"
3. Lugosi's Murder Legendre
4. Zombie son Noble Johnson
5. Film involving nightclub zombies
6. Ian Keith seeks blood transfusions from his victims
7. Animated feature with zombie aviators
8. Dean Jagger discovers a secret to creating zombies
9. Martin and Lewis encounter Jack Lambert zombie
10. Mantan Moreland thinks he's a zombie
11. Secret cellar with basement graveyard of zombified men
12. Mad scientist reviving dead wife with soul transfers
13. "They're coming to get you Barbara"
14. Louie Nye is a horror host named Zombo
15. Leonard Nimoy appeared in this one
16. Zombies guard a sunken treasure chest from treasure seekers
17. Radioactive snake venom zombies
18. Woman scientist wants to control the world with zombies
19. The first monster musical
20. Space aliens from the moon take over deceased bodies to conquer Earth
21. Dan Blocker (Hoss from *Bonanza*) plays a zombie in a Three Stooges short
22. Gangsters become zombies when their brains are replaced with atomic energy
23. A horror movie crew is murdered one at a time by a zombie

A) Bowery at Midnight
B) King of the Zombies
C) Voodoo Man
D) The Ghost Breakers
E) Mad Monster Party
F) Revolt of the Zombies
G) Zombies of the Stratosphere
H) The Munsters
I) Revenge of the Zombies
J) Zombies of Mora Tau
K) Zombies on Broadway
L) Night of the Living Dead
M) I Eat Your Skin
N) I Walked with a Zombie
O) Teenage Zombies
P) Valley of the Zombies
Q) White Zombie
R) Scared Stiff
S) Invisible Invaders
T) Creature with the Atom Brain
U) Outer Space Jitters
V) The House of Seven Corpses
W) The Incredibly Strange Creatures Who Stopped Living and Became Mixed Up Zombies

Answers page 144

Bibliography/Source Materials

Considerable time and research go into a book like this. Most of these facts become common knowledge to an avid horror movie buff. However the following list of resources helped me immensely on this project.

Unsold TV Pilots by Lee Goldberg (Citadel Press, New York, N.Y., 1991)
The Encyclopedia of Fantastic Films by R.G. Young (Applause Books, New York, N.Y., 2000)
Hollywood Cauldron by Gregory William Mank (McFarland and Company Inc., Jefferson, North Carolina, 1994)
Creature Features: The Science Fiction, Fantasy and Horror Movie Guide by John Stanley (Berkley Boulevard Books, New York,N.Y, 1997, 2000)
Collecting Monsters of Film and TV Identification and Value Guide; Dana Cain (Krause Publications, Iola, Wisconsin, 1999)
The Amazing Colossal Book of Horror Trivia by Jonathan Malcom Lampley, Ken Beck and Jim Clark (Cumberland House, Nashville, TN, 1999)
The Horror Spoofs of Abbott and Costello by Jeffrey S. Miller (McFarland and Company Inc., Jefferson, North Carolina and London, 2000)
It Came From Bob's Basement by Burns and Michlig (Chronicle Books, San Francisco, 2000)
The Essential Monster Movie Guide by Stephen Jones (Billboard Books, New York, N.Y., 1999, 2000)
Paul Blaisdell Monster Maker by Randy Palmer (McFarland and Company Inc., Jefferson, North Carolina and London, 1997)
Hollywood's Classic Scream Queens 1930's (Midnight Marquee Press Inc., Baltimore, Maryland, 2000)
Keep Watching The Skies by Bill Warren (McFarland and Company Inc., Jefferson, North Carolina and London, 1982 and 1986)

Periodicals:
Scary Monsters (Dennis Druktenis Publishing)
Midnight Marquee (Gary J. Svehla, publisher)
Monsters From The Vault (Jim Clatterbaugh, publisher)
And of course the original *Famous Monsters of Filmland* (Warren Publishing) with Uncle Forry

ANSWER PAGES

Check your cape at the door with your wolfsbane and tana leaves.

Abbott And Costello Meet Frankenstein
1. The Brain of Frankenstein
2. Ian Keith
3. True
4. Dracula's image in a mirror
5. True
6. Abbott and Costello Meet the Killer Boris Karloff
7. MacDougal's House of Horrors
8. Cat People, Curse of the Cat People
9. True
10. Dr. Lejos
11. Patricia Morrison
12. Lon Chaney, Jr.
13. The Invisible Man
14. Boris Karloff

Abbott And Costello Match
1. Bud Abbott (E)
2. Lou Costello (H)
3. Bud Abbott (A)
4. Lou Costello (G)
5. Bud Abbott (D)
6. Bud Abbott (C)
7. Bud Abbott (G)
8. Lou Costello (F)
9. Lou Costello (A)
10. Lou Costello (B)
11. Bud Abbott (H)
12. Lou Costello (E)
13. Bud Abbott (B)
14. Lou Costello (D)
15. Bud Abbott (F)
16. Lou Costello (C)

Assorted Horrors
1. Curse of the Undead
2. Giant from the Unknown
3. Cult of the Cobra
4. Rondo Hatton
5. The Face of Marble
6. Dr. X, The Most Dangerous Game, The Vampire Bat, The Mystery of the Wax Museum, Black Moon and The Clairvoyant
7. Elizabeth Russell
8. Konga
9. Aldetha Teech
10. The Vulture
11. I Married A Monster from Outer Space
12. Bride of the Gorilla
13. Monster on the Campus
14. Unearthly Stranger
15. Monster from Green Hell
16. Four Sided Triangle
17. The Flesh Eaters
18. Attack of the Crab Monsters
19. The Supremes
20. Dead of Night
21. Comin' Round the Mountain
22. One Million B. C.
23. The controversy over the battle scene involving the Tegu lizard's death with the baby dwarf alligator

Creature from the Black Lagoon
1. Ben Chapman
2. Ricou Browning
3. Creature from the Black Lagoon, Revenge of the Creature, The Creature Walks Among Us
4. Tom Hennesey
5. Julia Adams, Lori Nelson and Leigh Snowden
6. Don Megowan
7. Revenge of the Creature
8. Mechanix Illustrated Digest
9. The Colgate Comedy Hour
10. Glenn Strange
11. 3-D
12. Jack Arnold
13. True, an aquarium toy from Penn-Plax
14. The Seven Year Itch
15. Wakulla Springs (alt. spelling Wacola), Florida
16. Millicent Patrick
17. The Rita
18. Lucas
19. Henry Mancini, Hans J. Salter, and Herman Stein
20. Revenge of the Creature
21. Uncle Gilbert
22. King Kong
23. Rotonone

Dinomania
1. Dinosaurus
2. The Giant Behemoth
3. The Land Unknown
4. Tarzan's Desert Mystery
5. King Dinosaur
6. Unknown Island
7. Prehysteria
8. Baby: Secret of the Lost Legend
9. Beast of Hollow Mountain
10. Journey to the Beginning of Time
11. When Dinosaurs Ruled the Earth

Dracula
1. Renfield (Dwight Frye)
2. Tod Browning
3. Nosferatu A Symphony of Terror
4. Gloria Holden
5. Son of Dracula
6. Horror of Dracula
7. Brides of Dracula
8. Return of Dracula
9. Dracula—Prince of Darkness
10. Dracula Has Risen from the Grave
11. Blacula
12. Dracula A.D. 1972

For Monster Boomers Only
1. John Zacherle
2. Famous Monsters of Filmland
3. Aurora
4. Frankenstein
5. Monster Mash
6. The Munsters
7. Vampira
8. Quisp
9. The Addams Family
10. Alfred Hitchcock Presents
11. Barnabas Collins
12. The Forms of Things Unknown
13. Peter Lorre
14. William Castle
15. Spike Jones in Stereo
16. Strange Paradise
17. Lizard's Leg and Owlet's Wing
18. Don Post
19. Tor Johnson
20. Count Chocula, Frankenberry, Boo Berry, Yummy Mummy and Fruit Brute
21. Castle Films
22. Boris Karloff
23. Boris Karloff's Tales of Mystery
24. Frankenstein
25. The Monster
26. Earth vs. The Spider
27. EC Comics
28. The Munsters Coach, The Dragula Dragster
29. James Bama
30. American Bandstand (Dick Clark introduced him)
31. Horrible Herman
32. Shock Monster
33. The Munsters
34. Spook Stories

Godzilla and Friends
1. Pee Wee's Big Adventure
2. Blue Oyster Cult
3. Godzilla vs. the Sea Monster
4. Gigantis the Fire Monster. Godzilla was originally killed in the first film. Since there was no explanation for his return this was another Godzilla or Gigantis all along.
5. Rodan
6. Ghidrah the Three Headed Monster
7. Godzilla vs. the Bionic Monster
8. King Seesar
9. King Kong vs. Godzilla
10. Destroy All Monsters
11. Monster Zero. Nick Adams was also in Frankenstein Conquers the World.
12. Son of Godzilla
13. Minya
14. Raymond Burr
15. Godzilla (1998)
16. Mothra

Horrific Commercials
1. Honey Nut Cheerios
2. Volkswagen
3. A-1 Steak Sauce
4. Taco Bell
5. Ronson Comet Lighter
6. Peter Lorre
7. Right Guard
8. Reese's Peanut Butter Cup
9. Pepsi Cola (Joan Crawford was a spokesperson for Pepsi and her husband was the acting president at the time.)

10. Hostess Cupcakes
11. Dr. Jekyll and Mr. Hyde
12. Shasta Orange Soda
13. Dolly Madison
14. Basil Rathbone
15. Cheerios
16. The Frankenstein monster
17. Vincent Price
18. Godzilla

Invisibly Transparent
1. The Invisible Man
2. Boris Karloff
3. Vincent Price
4. Virginia Bruce
5. Jon Hall
6. Memoirs of an Invisible Man
7. Mad Monster Party
8. Abbott and Costello Meet the Invisible Man
9. The Amazing Transparent Man
10. The Invisible Monster

Jungle Madness
1. The Disembodied
2. Bela Lugosi Meets a Brooklyn Gorilla
3. Jungle Captive
4. From Hell It Came
5. The Bride and the Beast
6. Africa Screams
7. Jungle Moon Men

Monster Anagrams
1. House of Dracula
2. The Unearthly
3. Gothic
4. Bates Motel
5. The Neanderthal Man
6. Murders in the Zoo
7. Spider Baby
8. The Ape Man
9. Pharoah's Curse
10. Beware the Blob

Monster Beach Party
1. Bikini Beach
2. Peter Lorre
3. Vincent Price
4. Basil Rathbone
5. The Beach Girls and the Monster
6. Beach Blanket Bingo
7. The Horror of Party Beach
8. The Crawling Hand
9. The Monster That Challenged the World
10. Susan Hart
11. Monster of Piedras Blancas
12. Jaws
13. How to Stuff a Wild Bikini

Monster Movie Within a Movie
1. Attack of the Puppet People
2. The Amazing Colossal Man
3. Mant
4. I Was a Teenage Frankenstein
5. Invasion of the Saucer Men
6. Abbott and Costello Meet Frankenstein
7. The Howling
8. The Mummy (1959)
9. The Corpse Vanishes
10. It Came from Beneath the Sea
11. Night of the Living Dead
12. Dementia 13
13. Mrs. Doubtfire
14. The Majestic
15. The Blob
16. 1984
17. Invasion of the Body Snatchers
18. This Island Earth
19. Them
20. Way Way Out
21. Godzilla 1985

Monster Toys
1. Marx Windup Frankenstein
2. Soakies
3. Terror Tales
4. Herman Munster Talking Hand Puppet
5. True
6. The Creature, The Mummy, The Hunchback, The Wolfman, The Phantom of the Opera and Frankenstein.
7. Barnabas Collins
8. Big Frankie
9. Blushing Frankenstein
10. Green Ghost
11. Mars Attacks
12. Great Garlu
13. Ben Cooper
14. Creature from the Black Lagoon
15. Monster Old Maid
16. Pez

Monster Who Am I ?
1. The Maze
2. Return of the Fly
3. Dick Miller
4. Veronica Carlson
5. Son of Frankenstein
6. The She Creature
7. Mantan Moreland
8. Forrest J Ackerman
9. Buster Crabbe
10. Laird Cregar
11. Robert Clarke
12. Whit Bissell
13. Richard Kiel
14. Bronson Canyon

Monstrous Props
1. Dr. Zorba's portrait
2. The Land Unknown
3. Queen of Outer Space
4. The Monster of Piedras Blancas
5. Missile to the Moon
6. Wake of the Red Witch
7. The Incredible Shrinking Man
8. The Phantom Empire
9. Radar Men from the Moon
10. Creation of the Humanoids
11. The Terror
12. You'll Find Out
13. Dracula (1931)
14. The Rocket Man
15. Bedlam
16. Condemned to Live

Monsterous Sports Figures
1. Joe Bonomo
2. Rosey Grier
3. David Prowse, his first time as the monster was in Casino Royale followed by The Horror of Frankenstein and Frankenstein and the Monster from Hell
4. Primo Camera
5. Leo Durocher
6. Buddy Baer
7. Dwayne Johnson (The Rock), first appeared in The Mummy Returns and as the same character in The Scorpion King
8. The Swedish Angel
9. Steve Reeves
10. Johnny Weissmuller (Tarzan in Tarzan's Desert Mystery, Jungle Jim in Jungle Manhunt and Jungle Jim the TV series)

Robots/Mechanical Marvels
1. Kronos
2. The Mysterians
3. 2001: A Space Odyssey
4. Hal
5. Ro-Man
6. Robby the Robot
7. Gort
8. The Iron Giant
9. Devil Girl from Mars
10. R2D2 and C3-PO
11. Twiki
12. Colossus of New York
13. Tobor The Great
14. Colossus The Forbin Project
15. The Bowery Boys Meet the Monsters
16. Dr. Goldfoot and the Bikini Machine
17. It's Only Money
18. Target Earth
19. The Daleks
20. Westworld
21. THX-1138

Sci-Fi /Comedy Horrors
1. Rowan and Martin
2. The Ghost and Mr. Chicken
3. Laurel and Hardy
4. Blondie Has Servant Trouble
5. Peter Lorre
6. You'll Find Out
7. Visit to a Small Planet
8. The Private Eyes
9. My Favorite Spy
10. Scared Stiff
11. The Ritz Brothers
12. Ensign Pulver
13. The 30 Foot Bride of Candy Rock
14. Olsen and Johnson
15. Whistling in the Dark
16. Bela Lugosi Meets a Brooklyn Gorilla
17. Blackbeard's Ghost
18. The Ghost Breakers
19. Monkey Business
20. Hysterical
21. Tickle Me
22. The Burbs
23. Saturday the 14th
24. Mickey Rooney
25. Topper Returns

26. The Comedy of Terrors
27. The Three Stooges in Orbit
28. Space Master X-7
29. The Ritz Brothers
30. Joe E. Brown
31. Babes in Toyland or March of the Wooden Soldiers

Simians
1. King Kong Lives
2. Willis O'Brien
3. Planet of the Apes
4. APE
5. The Monkey's Paw
6. Captive Wild Woman, Jungle Woman
7. Gorilla at Large
8. The Ghost Busters
9. Konga
10. Mighty Joe Young
11. Beneath the Planet of the Apes
12. King Kong vs. Godzilla
13. Son of Kong
14. Phantom of the Rue Morgue
15. The Mighty Gorga
16. Killer Ape
17. Dr. Renault's Secret
18. Mark of the Gorilla

Spacecraft
1. Jupiter Two
2. Discovery 1
3. Rocketship X-M
4. Nostromo
5. Spindrift
6. UFO
7. The Galileo Seven
8. Fireball XL-5
9. Spacemaster X-7
10. The Death Star
11. Dark Star
12. The Millenium Falcon
13. X-Wing

Spooky Radio
1. Orson Welles (War of the Worlds)
2. Inner Sanctum
3. Suspense
4. Space Patrol
5. Lights Out
6. Bill Cosby
7. The Hermit's Cave
8. The Weird Circle
9. Richard Denning
10. Bela Lugosi and Boris Karloff

Star Treatment
1. Vincent Price/Christopher Lee
2. Bela Lugosi
3. Eight: Gift of Gab, The Black Cat, The Raven, Son of Frankenstein, The Invisible Ray, Black Friday, You'll Find Out, The Body Snatcher
4. True
5. The Return of Dr. X
6. The Night Walker
7. Richard Denning
8. Supernatural
9. Lon Chaney, Sr., Lon Chaney, Jr., Boris Karloff and Bela Lugosi
10. A Christmas Carol or Scrooge
11. John Carradine
12. Red Planet Mars, Beginning of the End, Killers from Space and It Conquered the World
13. James Whale
14. Tor Johnson
15. Another Saturday Night
16. Rondo Hatton
17. Leo G. Carroll
18. Phantom of the Opera
19. Forbidden Planet
20. Peter Lorre
21. William Castle
22. Gale Sondergaard
23. Claude Rains
24. Bob Burns
25. Caroline Munro
26. Irving Pichel
27. Kenneth Strickfaden
28. Charles Herbert
29. Boris Karloff's daughter Sara
30. Danny DeVito (Jack the Bear)
31. John Beal
32. Little Shop of Horrors
33. Carla Laemmle

34. Roy Scheider
35. Craig T. Nelson
36. Bela Lugosi
37. The producers of the film: Ernest B. Schoedsack and Merian C. Cooper
38. Hazel Court
39. Barbara Leigh
40. Francis X. Bushman
41. In real life she was his second wife
42. Boris Karloff
43. Cecil B. DeMille
44. Roland West
45. Ginger Rogers
46. James Whale
47. Bela Lugosi
48. Gary Clarke
49. First National (Warner Bros.)
50. Scared to Death

To Bee Or Not To Bee
1. The Wasp Woman
2. The Bees
3. Invasion of the Bee Girls
4. ZZZZZ
5. Giant African wasps
6. The Swarm
7. Mysterious Island
8. The Food of the Gods
9. Honey I Shrunk the Kids
10. Sinbad and the Eye of the Tiger
11. The Deadly Bees
12. Killer Bees
13. The Savage Bees

TV Horrors Dark Shadows
1. ABC
2. B (June 27, 1966)
3. Dan Curtis
4. In a dream
5. Collingwood
6. Victoria Winters
7. Barnabas Collins
8. Waves crashing on the rocks
9. Angelique
10. Grayson Hall and Barbara Steele
11. Quentin Collins
12. Widow's Hill
13. Robert Cobert
14. Joan Bennett
15. Two (House of Dark Shadows and Night of Dark Shadows)

16. The Blue Whale
17. The Strange Case of Dr. Jekyll and Mr. Hyde
18. C (Thayer David)
19. Barnabas

TV Terrors
1. Cleopatra
2. "You rang"
3. Marie Antoinette
4. Boris Karloff's Thriller
5. Vincent Price
6. Count Istvan Teleky
7. Old man Rimshaw
8. Amos Chantz
9. A headless ghost (but actually just a headless mannequin)
10. A Gremlin
11. "The Grim Reaper"
12. Kolchak The Night Stalker ("The Trevi Collection")
13. Woof Woof
14. Dry Bones
15. Roald Dahl
16. My Living Doll
17. John Newland
18. 13 Demon Street
19. The Veil (Hosted by Boris Karloff)
20. Alfred Hitchcock Presents
21. Hayata
22. Eiji Tsuburaya
23. The Standells

Way Out There
1. The Lions Head Inn
2. Wallace Ford
3. Teenagers from Outer Space
4. The She Creature
5. Man in the Attic
6. Destination Moon
7. Ann Robinson
8. Professor Lampini, George Zucco
9. Neustadt Prison
10. Gone With the Wind (the burning of Atlanta)
11. H.G. Wells
12. Tante Berthe's Café
13. Superstition Vs. Reason and Fact
14. Mapleton Cemetery
15. Plato Zorba
16. The Monkees
17. Phoebe (actress Joan Marshall)
18. Gocko
19. Frankenstein Meets the Space Monster
20. Davanna
21. John Carradine
22. Cliff Robertson
23. The Star of India necklace
24. Molly Malone
25. Basil Rathbone
26. The Mummy (1932) with Boris Karloff on the poster.
27. The name is George Waggner, the director of The Wolfman
28. Dr. Demento

Werewolves
1. Werewolf of London
2. Maria Ouspenskaya
3. Cry of the Werewolf
4. Matt Willis
5. She Wolf of London
6. Curse of the Werewolf
7. Werewolf in a Girls Dormitory
8. The Werewolf
9. House of Dracula
10. Werewolves on Wheels

What's In Common With
1. Maila Nurmi (Vampira)
2. Characters portrayed by Warner Oland
3. Tor Johnson
4. Michael Gough starred in and played Alfred the butler in the Batman films
5. Robert Lowery starred in and portrayed Batman in one of the 1940s serials
6. Al Lewis
7. All portrayed Hercules
8. They portrayed Jack the Ripper
9. The film House of Wax
10. David Hedison played Felix Leiter in two Bond films. He was in the TV series Voyage to the Bottom of the Sea
11. All portrayed Lily Munster
12. All starred as Sinbad
13. Clint Eastwood was in films/TV series
14. David Prowse was in each film
15. All portrayed Nosferatu
16. All portrayed Captain Nemo
17. Forrest J Ackerman had cameos in them
18. All shared the last name Frankenstein
19. All portrayed Sherlock Holmes
20. All portrayed the Phantom of the Opera
21. Starred in or directed by Charles Laughton
22. Portrayed Fu Manchu
23. Portrayed Van Helsing
24. John Dierkes played in each film
25. They all have a connection with gremlins
26. The Munsters' house can be seen in each
27. They were each portrayed by Ted Cassidy

Photo ID Answers

Frontispiece: Adventures of Sherlock Holmes
Table of Contents: Altered States
14: Bride of Frankenstein
16: The Fearless Vampire Killers
17: Kirk Alyn
18: Top: Bud Westmore, Bottom: Rick Baker
20: The Day the Earth Stood Still
22: Black Cat: Karloff, Ulmer, Wells, Manners
24: The Bowery Boys Meet the Monsters
26: Top to Bottom: Bernard Herrmann, Miklos Rozsa, Max Steiner
29: Bela Lugosi as Dracula
31: Julia Adams
32: The Giant Behemoth
33: Horror of Dracula
34: Blossom Rock, Jackie Coogan; The Addams Family
35: The Phantom of the Opera (Chaney)
40: Mill of Stone Women
43: The Innocents
44: Daughter of Dr. Jekyll
46: The Killer Shrews
47: Attack of the Giant Leeches
52: The Black Sleep
53: 4D Man
54: The Amazing Colossal Man
55: The Horror of Party Beach
56: Abbott and Costello Meet the Invisible Man
57: Invisible Man Returns
58: King Kong
59: Dr. Jekyll, Fredric March
60: The Mole People
62: From Hell It Came
67: The Magic Sword
69: The Tingler, 13 Ghosts
71: Tales of Terror
72: The Ghost in the Invisible Bikini
73: The Creeping Terror
74: Service DeLuxe
79: Top: Forbidden Planet
80: Johan Carradine as Dracula from House of Dracula
84: Plan 9 From Outer Space
86: Invasion of the Saucer Men
87: Plan 9 From Outer Space
89: The Phantom of Crestwood
90: Two on a Guillotine
91: Bride of Frankenstein: Clive, Lanchester
92: Mysterious Island
93: Outer Limits
94: The She Creature
95: The Day the World Ended
96: Mad Monster
97: Jason and the Argonauts
100: You'll Find Out
102: Mighty Joe Young
103: Peter Cushing and Carrie Fisher in Star Wars
104: Zita Johann, The Mummy
107: The Raven (1935)
108: War Gods of the Deep
109: The Raven (1963)
110: The Wasp Woman
111: Sir Graves Ghastly
113: Jonathan Frid as Barnabus Collins
114: Left: Nicholas Hormann, as Vorvon in "Space Vampire" Right: James Fairfax, Ray Montgomery and Jon Hall meet some TV horrors in Ramar of the Jungle
116: Top: Carolyn Jones, The Addams Family
Middle: Bob Cummings and Julie Newmar
Bottom: William Shatner Twilight Zone
117: Jim Nabors, Andy Griffith and Don Knotts in "Haunted House"
118: The Monster That Challenged the World
119: The Vampire's Ghost
120: Fred Gwynne as Herman Munster
122: Werewolf of London
123. Barbara Steele
124: The 27th Day
126: The Beginning of the End
128: Daddy-O; Bottom: The Haunted Palace
129: Zombies of Mora Tau

AKA
1. L
2. A
3. H
4. F
5. D
6. B
7. C
8. G
9. E
10. I
11. K
12. J
13. M
14. N

Alien Races
1. J
2. F
3. H
4. B
5. C
6. D
7. E
8. G
9. I
10. K
11. A

Alternate Film Titles
1. C
2. D
3. F
4. A
5. H
6. N
7. B
8. J
9. O
10. G
11. P
12. M
13. K
14. L
15. I
16. E

Amazing Heroes
1. E
2. H
3. A
4. K
5. B
6. D
7. I
8. F
9. G
10. L
11. M
12. N
13. O
14. Q
15. R
16. P
17. S
18. J
19. C
20. T

Artists and Monsters
1. E
2. H
3. L
4. D
5. G
6. F
7. J
8. A
9. M
10. I
11. B
12. K
13. C
14. O
15. N
16. P

B-Movie Greats
1. J
2. O
3. I
4. C
5. F
6. Q
7. L
8. E
9. R
10. S
11. W
12. T
13. B
14. G
15. V
16. D
17. H
18. U
19. M
20. X
21. N
22. A
23. P
24. Y
25. K

Ballyhoo
1. F
2. K
3. O
4. B
5. G
6. J
7. D
8. H
9. A
10. L
11. E
12. N
13. C
14. M
15. I
16. P
17. Q

Behind the Screams
1. E
2. F
3. B
4. I
5. H
6. A
7. G
8. C
9. D
10. K
11. M
12. J
13. L

Body Parts
1. E
2. D
3. G
4. J
5. H
6. M
7. A
8. L
9. F
10. I
11. C
12. N
13. K
14. P
15. O
16. B

The Boys Are Back In Town
1. E
2. J
3. D
4. K
5. A
6. I
7. H
8. G
9. B
10. L
11. M
12. C
13. F

Cartoon Creeps
1. E
2. D
3. A
4. F
5. P
6. H
7. I
8. Q
9. M
10. K
11. G
12. N
13. O
14. J
15. L
16. C
17. B

Composing Thoughts
1. I
2. L
3. K
4. J
5. G
6. C
7. M
8. F
9. B
10. N
11. E
12. D
13. H
14. A

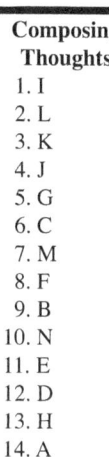

of Horror, Fantasy and Sci-Fi Movie Trivia

Creature Features/ Double Features
1. Q
2. G
3. X
4. J
5. C
6. Y
7. A
8. W
9. D
10. F
11. I
12. K
13. M
14. L
15. H
16. P
17. N
18. O
19. Z
20. R
21. T
22. U
23. S
24. V
25. B
26. E

Creepy Houses and Spooky Locations
1. F
2. I
3. G
4. H
5. E
6. U
7. A and J
8. Q
9. C
10. D
11. B
12. P
13. S
14. K
15. R
16. L
17. M
18. O
19. N
20. A
21. W
22. T
23. X

Family Ties
1. D
2. K
3. G
4. N
5. A
6. M
7. E
8. C
9. B
10. F
11. H
12. I
13. L
14. P
15. O

Fantastic Phantoms
1. G
2. F
3. H
4. I
5. C
6. A
7. E
8. B
9. D
10. L
11. J
12. K

Film Stars With Elvis
1. C
2. E
3. D
4. D
5. E
6. G
7. F or O
8. A
9. K
10. D
11. Q
12. L
13. N
14. R
15. M
16. M
17. A
18. F
19. G or H
20. O
21. S
22. I
23. J
24. P
25. U
26. B

Foreign Horrors
1. F
2. H
3. D
4. B
5. E
6. A
7. I
8. G
9. C
10. K
11. J
12. L

Frankenstein By Any Other Name
1. Q
2. I
3. M
4. O
5. D
6. A
7. F
8. B
9. H
10. K
11. E
12. C
13. L
14. G
15. J
16. N
17. P

Game Show of Horrors
1. B E or J
2. F
3. B E or J
4. A or H
5. B E or J
6. C
7. D
8. A or H
9. G
10. I
11. K

Ghosts
1. F
2. J
3. D
4. A
5. H
6. B
7. M
8. C
9. I
10. E
11. N
12. G
13. K
14. O
15. L

Ghouls Just Want To Have Fun
1. E
2. G
3. J
4. R
5. K
6. L
7. C
8. O
9. M
10. D
11. N
12. A
13. B
14. I
15. F
16. Q
17. H
18. P

Great Special Effects
1. M
2. K
3. I
4. B
5. A
6. L
7. J
8. G
9. H
10. D
11. E
12. C
13. F
14. N

Halloween Haunts
1. H
2. E
3. B
4. F
5. A
6. C
7. G
8. I
9. K
10. M
11. N
12. J
13. O
14. L
15. P
16. D
17. Q
18. R

Horror Actors' Last Roles
1. J
2. G
3. F
4. B
5. H or M
6. E
7. A
8. I
9. K
10. C
11. L
12. D
13. H or M
14. N
15. Q
16. P
17. O

How to Destroy a Monster
1. T
2. R
3. O
4. K
5. P
6. V
7. W
8. L
9. B
10. A
11. D
12. C
13. E
14. Y
15. Q
16. U
17. S
18. H
19. M
20. X
21. F
22. G
23. J
24. N
25. I

It Landed On The Cutting Room Floor
1. C
2. F
3. D
4. H
5. K
6. E
7. I
8. B
9. A
10. M
11. G
12. L
13. J
14. N

John Agar
1. E
2. K
3. M
4. G
5. J
6. P
7. B
8. L
9. Q
10. A
11. R
12. C
13. N
14. H
15. F
16. D
17. I
18. O

Horrible Headlines
1. E
2. D
3. K
4. B
5. Q
6. C
7. J
8. A
9. F
10. I
11. L
12. M
13. O
14. H
15. R
16. N
17. P
18. G
19. S
20. T

How to Become a Monster
1. L
2. M
3. K
4. P
5. N
6. I
7. F
8. O
9. A
10. C
11. B
12. H
13. G
14. D
15. E
16. J

I Wore a Monster Costume
1. D
2. B
3. L
4. K
5. I
6. M
7. J
8. F
9. H
10. G
11. C
12. A
13. E
14. P
15. O
16. N

Jekyll and Hyde
1. I
2. K
3. M
4. C
5. H
6. J
7. B
8. L
9. G
10. N
11. A
12. D
13. O
14. E
15. F
16. P

Just Mad About Karloff
1. K
2. L
3. G
4. M
5. B
6. N
7. H
8. A
9. O
10. P
11. I
12. Q
13. C
14. R
15. E
16. S
17. T
18. J
19. F
20. D
21. U

Literally Speaking
1. I and B2
2. M and A1
3. P and F6
4. E and I9
5. B and H8
6. A and D4
7. C and L12
8. H and M13
9. D and N14
10. F and K11
11. K and O15
12. N and P16
13. G and G7
14. O and E5
15. L and J10
16. J and C3

Made For TV Sci-Fi/Horror/Fantasy
1. H
2. L
3. K
4. B
5. F
6. A
7. I
8. D
9. E
10. M
11. C
12. N
13. O
14. G
15. J
16. P
17. Q

A Magic Moment
1. C
2. G
3. K
4. H
5. I
6. B
7. D
8. J
9. F
10. E
11. A

Monster Ad Campaign
1. N
2. D
3. R
4. T
5. C
6. L
7. P
8. A
9. I
10. F
11. J
12. S
13. E
14. B
15. G
16. M
17. K
18. O
19. H
20. Q
21. U
22. V
23. W

Monster Anthologies
1. F
2. A
3. G
4. B
5. H
6. E
7. D
8. J
9. K
10. C
11. M
12. I
13. L
14. N
15. Q
16. O
17. P
18. R

Monster Character Traits
1. N
2. G
3. J
4. L
5. P
6. D
7. F
8. I
9. A
10. B
11. E
12. K
13. C
14. M
15. H
16. R
17. Q
18. O

Monster Film Stars Debuts
1. E
2. F
3. M
4. H
5. I
6. A
7. B
8. C
9. D
10. G
11. L
12. J
13. K
14. O
15. Q
16. P
17. R
18. N

Monster Movie Quotes
1. O
2. N
3. H
4. D or Q
5. S
6. B
7. J
8. A
9. D or Q
10. C
11. E
12. F
13. I
14. K
15. L
16. G
17. M
18. P
19. R
20. T
21. U

Monster Pop
1. I
2. K
3. J
4. T
5. Q
6. L
7. P
8. Y
9. A
10. N
11. U
12. D
13. B
14. O
15. C
16. F
17. E
18. G
19. H
20. M
21. R
22. X
23. W
24. Z
25. V
26. S

Monster Star Quotes
1. C
2. H
3. D
4. A
5. E
6. F
7. G (Karloff on Val Lewton)
8. B
9. I
10. J
11. K

Monstrous Bloopers
1. C
2. J
3. E
4. H
5. D
6. G
7. I
8. A
9. F
10. B

Monstrous Movie Songs
1. K
2. H
3. E
4. T
5. O
6. B
7. C
8. F
9. G
10. P
11. L
12. D
13. N
14. Q
15. A
16. I
17. M
18. S
19. R
20. J
21. Z
22. W
23. U
24. X
25. Y
26. V

Monstrous Remakes
1. E
2. F
3. H
4. G
5. C
6. A
7. B
8. D
9. I
10. J

Mummy's the Word
1. G
2. O
3. Q
4. A
5. F
6. I
7. K
8. L
9. P
10. B
11. H
12. N
13. E
14. D
15. C
16. J
17. M

Mysterious Plots
1. H
2. K
3. E
4. G
5. C
6. I
7. A
8. B
9. F
10. L
11. J
12. D
13. M
14. N

No Bones About It
1. C
2. I
3. F
4. M
5. H
6. A
7. Q
8. D
9. B
10. N
11. K
12. E
13. P
14. O
15. L
16. G
17. J

Occupational Pursuits
1. G
2. A
3. B
4. J
5. C
6. H
7. I
8. E
9. F
10. D
11. K
12. L
13. M
14. N
15. O

On a Monster Island with You
1. I
2. D
3. A
4. E
5. J
6. B
7. F
8. L
9. C
10. H
11. K
12. G
13. M

The Outer Limits
1. C
2. F
3. B
4. H
5. I
6. D
7. A
8. J
9. E
10. G
11. K
12. O
13. L
14. M
15. Q
16. P
17. N
18. R
19. T
20. S
21. V
22. U
23. W

Paul Blaisdell
1. D
2. C
3. J
4. K
5. F
6. A or Q
7. G
8. E
9. L
10. A or Q
11. M
12. N
13. H
14. I
15. O
16. P
17. B
18. S
19. R

PRC/ Monogram Madness
1. A
2. F
3. H
4. C
5. G
6. D
7. M
8. O
9. L
10. K
11. J
12. N
13. B
14. I
15. E

Ray Harryhausen
1. F
2. B
3. K
4. M
5. H
6. B
7. C
8. A
9. D
10. C
11. E
12. G
13. E
14. D
15. J
16. D
17. I
18. G
19. L
20. E

Scream Queens
1. F
2. C
3. I
4. H
5. O
6. J
7. N
8. L
9. M
10. K
11. A
12. R
13. T
14. B
15. P
16. S
17. E
18. Q
19. G
20. D
21. U

Teenage Horrors
1. L
2. P
3. N
4. G
5. I
6. A
7. K
8. B
9. M
10. C
11. D
12. G or R or A
13. E
14. H
15. O
16. F
17. Q
18. J

of Horror, Fantasy and Sci-Fi Movie Trivia

Titans of Horror
1. H
2. E
3. F
4. L
5. B
6. N
7. K
8. O
9. M
10. G
11. I
12. J
13. D
14. P
15. A
16. C

TV Horror Hosts
1. E
2. Q
3. O
4. P
5. M
6. K
7. L
8. N
9. H
10. B
11. I
12. J
13. G
14. D
15. C
16. A
17. F
18. R

Television Horrors
1. J
2. N
3. L
4. C
5. Q
6. P
7. A
8. B
9. G
10. D
11. O
12. M
13. T
14. E or H
15. I
16. R
17. V
18. F
19. S
20. H or E
21. U
22. K
23. Y
24. Z
25. X
26. W

TV Horrors Out of This World Pilots
1. D
2. G
3. I
4. E
5. N
6. C
7. H
8. A
9. J
10. F
11. M
12. K
13. L
14. B
15. P
16. O

Underwater Monstrosities
1. E
2. H
3. K
4. J
5. I
6. B
7. C
8. D
9. A
10. F
11. G
12. N
13. L
14. M

Vampires
1. K
2. H or D
3. A
4. F
5. B
6. I
7. C
8. D or H
9. E
10. M
11. G
12. J
13. N
14. O
15. L
16. P

Variety of Horrors
1. D
2. G
3. H
4. I
5. A
6. F
7. C
8. E
9. B
10. J
11. L
12. O
13. K
14. M
15. N
16. P
17. Q

What A Steele
1. K
2. H
3. I
4. E
5. F
6. G
7. A
8. L
9. J
10. D
11. M
12. C
13. B

What's in a Number?
1. H
2. I
3. E
4. J
5. B
6. F
7. D
8. G
9. C
10. M
11. O
12. N
13. A
14. L
15. K

Where Monsters Die
1. G
2. I
3. H
4. B
5. E
6. C
7. J
8. F
9. D
10. A
11. L
12. K

The Year Is
1. D (1968)
2. N (1957)
3. B (1966)
4. O (1951)
5. L (1931)
6. C (1925)
7. G (1961)
8. E (1950)
9. F (1974)
10. K (1954)
11. M (1993)
12. H (1943)
13. J (1955)
14. A (1932)
15. I (1956)

You Know Bruno
1. C
2. G
3. D
4. F
5. H
6. E
7. A
8. B
9. I
10. J

Zombies
1. I
2. N
3. Q
4. D
5. K
6. P
7. E
8. F
9. R
10. B
11. A
12. C
13. L
14. H
15. G
16. J
17. M
18. O
19. W
20. S
21. U
22. T
23. V

About the Author

Keith Hedges is an avid monster movie buff as well as a local Elvis tribute artist. He resides in Indian Head, Maryland with his wife and son.

Hedges is working on a book of poetry of nostalgic remembrances and Christian themes.

Combining two loves–monsters and Elvis, Keith Hedges performs at FANEX 16.

If you enjoyed this book
check out our other
film-related titles at
www.midmar.com
or call or write for a free catalog
Midnight Marquee Press, Inc.
9721 Britinay Lane
Baltimore, MD 21234
410-665-1198
(8 a.m. until 6 p.m. EST)
or MMarquee@aol.com

www.ingramcontent.com/pod-product-compliance
Lightning Source LLC
Chambersburg PA
CBHW071502080526
44587CB00014B/2190